CW01638332

SHADY BIZZNESS

Life as Eminem's Bodyguard in an Industry of Paper Gangsters

by Byron "Big-Naz" Williams

Ecclesiastes 3:7

A time to tear;
a tear to sew;
a time to keep silence;
a time to speak.

FASTLIFE

Publication Data

Byron Williams, 1970 -

Shady Bizzness
by Byron "Big-Naz"Williams

Transcribed by Danielle P. Roberts
Photographs by Byron Williams

Biography

ISBN: 0-9767687-051798
1. Popular Music – promotions and publicity
2. Popular Culture
3. Music – Rap and Hip Hop

Printed in the USA

The following people/things made this book possible in one way or another (and listed in no particular order)

God Almighty
Mom and Dad
Jue-Jue my wife
Boo-Man my eldest
Brand-Brand my blessing child
Lil Buddy the monster baby
Grandma Rosetta and her prayers
Pastor Twymon
Rev. Livingston
Danielle Roberts
Adam Wolf Rogers
Stephanie Hammonds Attorney at law
Mark Hicks
Myron (Hustle Man) Williams
Shonda and her micro-recorder
Big Kenny
Sarge and Roe
Rock of J/A Security
Divine Culture Thee Intense M.F.
Randy Cooke
Frankie Biggz
E-Bone and Jamal Spivey
Chasco (Lunch Room Crew)
DASIT
Art Forest
Ganny & Pops
Jamal Stubbs & Hanif Stubbs

May they all rest in peace
My little cousin Joshua Jenkins
and Korupt's former bodyguard (Dwayne ìDrawsî Dupree)
My cousin Helen Ma Ghee
Ma Dear

Table of Contents

Byron Williams

About the Author

I've always considered myself privileged and blessed, even as a child. I was fortunate to have been raised by both parents in Detroit.They always provided me with the best things in life, from love to education. Although I wasn't an angel, I tried my best to stay out of trouble. My father has always preached to keep my name clean, because that's all a black man has. Fortunately, I followed his commands through proper discipline, which kept me on a straight-and-narrow path. I carried the burden of being the eldest of three sons. Therefore, I had to be a role model.

My mother instilled the fear of God in my heart and a never-quit attitude. I still carry those with me today. As an adolescent, I was always more mature than my peers. When they wanted to play games, I was out making money. I did everything from forming my own landscaping clientele to nursing the elderly. As I grew older, I grew competitive through sports. At the age of fourteen, I fell in love with basketball. Many people considered me a natural. I learned through watching my older cousin, Vernon, and later being forced to play in the big-fella games. Playing with the big guys prepared me for high school, where I broke many records. When my high school career ended, I earned the league MVP and a college scholarship. I had several different offers to play nationwide, but I chose to stay close to home. I attended Olivet College, which was a small Division 3 school and 90% white. Although there weren't many blacks, we were all close. I had no problem mingling with the whites because my high school was predominately white. I never worried about losing my identity. My family and friends made sure of that.

I was recruited as the No. 1 basketball player of the freshman class, not to mention the only black. I never experienced true racism until I reached college. Unfortunately, some of the guys on the basketball team had never been around black folks; this was a interesting experience. Being the only black guy on the team, I was always targeted to be the fall guy. However, I wasn't taking any bull, and I made sure that was known! During the next two years, campus racism intensified. The students tried to ignore the symptoms, but it only got worse. One night in April 1992, a white female was caught cheating on her boyfriend. Her boyfriend was a friend of two black student athletes who were with him on the night he discovered her unfaithfulness. When the white female noticed it was her boyfriend at the door with his two black friends, she panicked. Instead of her confessing that she was having sex with another guy at that moment, she created a diversion. One of which almost cost the two black males their lives! The white female called her fraternity brothers over to her dorm urgently, saying the black guys tried to rape her. She flat-out lied! Immediately, her twenty frat brothers rushed to the scene and attacked the two blacks. They had no idea what was going on! The other blacks caught wind of what was happening, and we all rushed downstairs to even the numbers. Before we realized it, we were in a racial riot, and the blacks were throwing the white frat boys through picture windows. The whites began to scurry as it became a fair fight. In racism no one wins. Finally, the state police and sheriff's deptartment showed up in riot gear, and the majority of the blacks were hauled off and blamed for the incident.

Later that night, another black senior and I took it upon ourselves to contact the press, although that wasn't our primary objective. We had called a few thugs from Detroit who agreed to shoot up the fraternity after setting the house afire. When the thugs showed up, they were disappointed that we had changed our plans. We decided to put Olivet College as a forerunner of black rights by demanding reprimands of discipline at a press conference. Unfortunately, Olivet decided not punish the fraternity for their wrongful behavior. Shortly after the press conference, we received death threats from the KKK, with attached literature. Minister Louis Farrakhan caught wind of our tribulations and advised us to get out of that hostile situation. After having gained much negative media exposure, Olivet College convinced another white female student to lie and say that I raped her. This was the college's tactic of trying to keep me quiet about the school's history of racism. The allegations were proven false within 24 hours. My counselor investigated the situation and found that I was home in Detroit at the day and time of the supposed incident. The College Board later apologized, but the damage was already done. I was truly hurt by that incident, and it could have ruined my life.

After taking my finals and earning my public relations degree (B.A.), it was impossible to start a career. Every time I would apply for a job, I was accused of being a troublemaker. My face was constantly seen in interviews, and people thought the blacks caused the Olivet Riot, but we were the resolution. They were ignorant about the facts, and instead of employment interviews being about the job, they would become interviews about the race riot. I would never get the job because the inter- viewers thought I would be a troublemaker or an agitator. I feel it's fair that people show mutual respect. But if someone does you wrong, it only comes back to him or her, and that's what people fail to realize. I believe that once a person proves himself or herself and fits in, then he or she should stand on his or her own merit.

In my past, I could have related to Slim, because I was a minority in a white-dominated situation. He feels that he belongs, and he is a good artist. Unfortunately, Slim also plays a role in a society that tells white lies and ruins peoples' lives when the shit is getting thick!

Byron Williams
E-mail: Bignaz228@aol.com

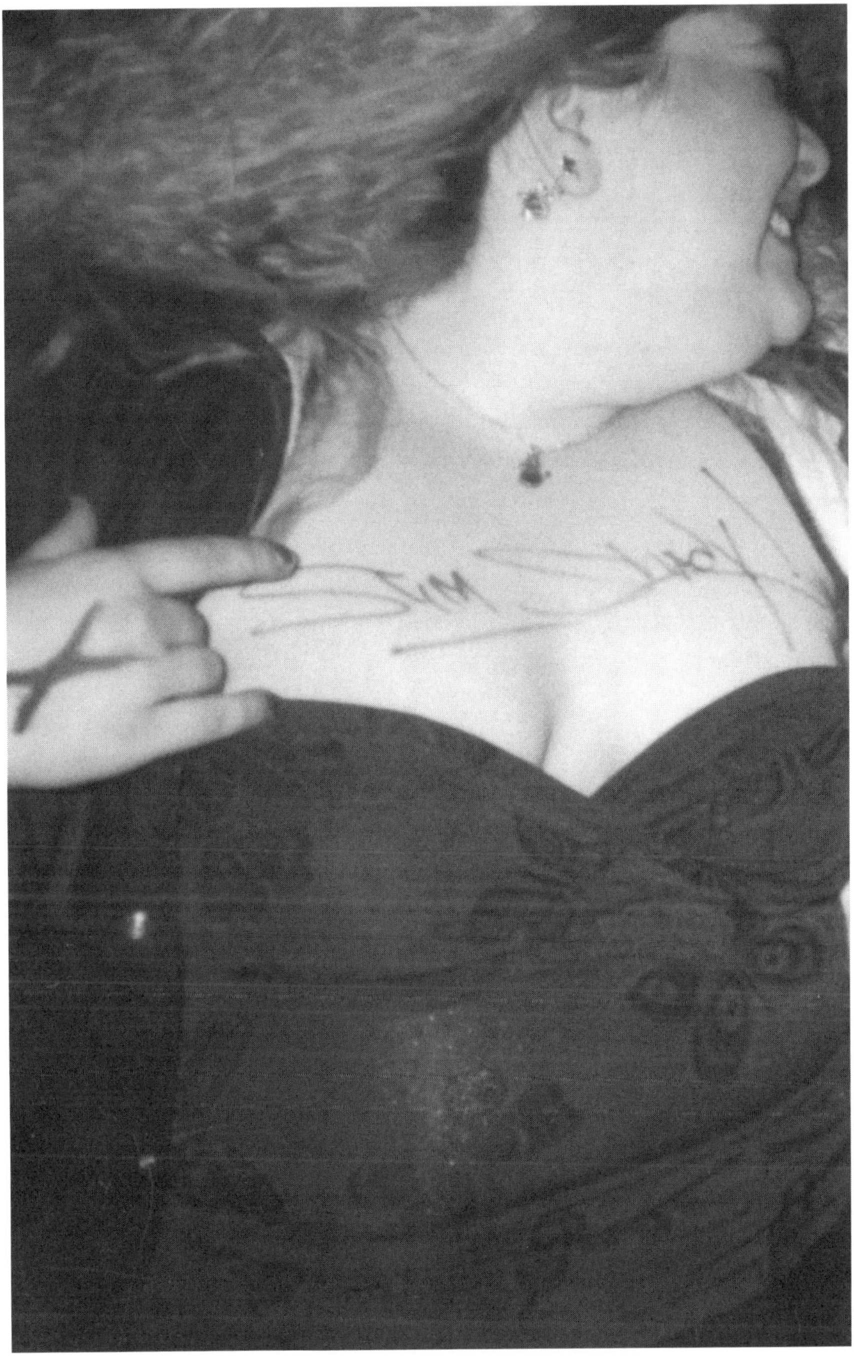

A diehard Slim Shady fan!

1

THE SLIM SHADY TOUR

History constantly repeats itself. Over the last eight years, I have fought lies against entities stronger than I. I thought working for Slim Shady would somehow be different, but I was wrong. I had no idea that I would be accused of STALKING the very man I protected, SLIM SHADY! There was a change of heart between Slim and I when he brandished his 9 mm and made threats against me. Unknown to Slim, I had my hand in my coat pocket holding a .40 cal.—praying not to take his life in selfdefense. We had been through too much for such a sour ending—or at least I thought.

How did Byron "Big Nasty"Williams hook up with Slim Shady? One night I was sitting downstairs in my new home watching an MTV special about Slim Shady. I had heard about him and figured he was probably just another Vanilla Ice. I watched his video and was into it, so I went looking for his CD. Since all of the stores were sold out, I said to myself, "This kid must really be hot!" Finally, I got the CD, and the next thing I knew that's all I was listening to on my way to work at GM every day. I told other people about it, but they would say, "Aw, that white boy, he's probably no different than Vanilla Ice." They didn't want to give him a chance and discredited him before checking him out. At the time, I was thinking, If this kid can make it, my groups can make it, too. I wasn't being hateful or anything, I just knew that my groups were as talented as he was, and with Slim being from Detroit maybe it would open up some doors for other groups. I had seen many failures trying to get a deal, and basically we were selling our product on the street. I had my own label, Big Willz, and it seemed like getting a major deal wasn't going to happen. By the time I met Slim, I had basically given up on this music thing and had pretty much settled on being an everyday Joe working at GM. It just seemed like every time I tried to get away from the music game, something would happen to pull me back in. I always did security on the side for some extra money, and on this particular night I got a call from crazy ass "Wolf," Adam Rogers, a street politician who knows a lot of people. I knew with him calling, something was about to happen. He told me that Slim was in town and needed some security for a rave party and asked if I would be interested. I told him that I wasn't really trying to get into anything to do with music at that time; I was frustrated with it and content with my job. But Wolf proceeded to talk me into checking it out, anyway. Later, Paul Rosenberg (Slim's manager and attorney) called me to ask me to be the security guy, trying—unsuccessfully—to impress me. He tried to get me to do three hours for $150, but I told him to give me $250, and I would cover him with a couple of my boys, and we agreed on that. I thought it would be a one-night deal. It was easy money. I guess Paul was impressed with everything we did because the next thing I knew he wanted me to go on tour with them. His request was on short notice, however, and I wasn't impressed. It seemed like the music business was trying to get a hold on me once again. I contemplated it and talked to my people about it, and they encouraged me. My man Art Forest, who runs the studio we record at, told me I would be a fool not to take the job. He said it didn't matter that I was security; he saw it as me getting my foot in the door. I had a long talk with my wife about it, and next thing I knew I was taking a leave of absence from GM and was packing my bags, not knowing whether my decision was going to hurt me or help me.

It was Wednesday, April 7, 1999, and the tour began. My first flight was the shittiest ever, and I think it was because of a woman; they had a woman piloting the plane, and she wasn't very good at it! I didn't have anyone to talk to, and I got the feeling that none of the other guys in Slim's crew wanted me there. I already was feeling guilty for leaving my family, particularly with a two-month-old baby, and my wife probably felt like a single parent. She is a strong woman, though, and has always been there for me. She remained supportive. As soon as we touched ground, I called all of my people to feel at home again. I felt proud of myself for being there. I wondered what to do next. I constantly read my Bible to remain focused, and I did that throughout the whole tour. Some of the shit I saw on that tour made me think I was working for the devil.

We did two shows in Chicago. The first show was mild, but prior to the second show Slim was drinking like a fish and doing all kinds of drugs, so at that point I knew I was in for a ride. I don't even know how he did the show. Some of his words were slurred, but he pulled through it. He must have done twenty stage dives that night, and I had to get him back on the stage, which wasn't easy while fighting twenty girls trying to rip his shirt off. I proved myself that first night, but I got no thanks or anything. I had to go introduce myself to people that night because no one had said anything to me yet. I didn't expect it, though, since security personnel always have the most responsibility and the least respect. After that, we headed to Pittsburgh.We were all getting acquainted, since it was the beginning of the tour and we didn't really know one other. Slim had Proof and DJ Head, and then there was Gus, the tour manager Billy, the production manager,G, the bus driver, and me.There was a real ethnic mix of characters. Gus was the cool white dude. Billy was a straight-up stoner and openly smoked everything under the sun, but he got his job done as long as you let him do his thing. Gus had been touring for fifteen years and was only thirty. Nothing impressed him. Basically, he just wanted to get the job done because he had seen everything. Proof, who is the best freestyle emcee in the world, was Slim's hype man and didn't drink or smoke at all before he began this tour. DJ Head and Billy were like Cheech and Chong on the tour, but Head always gave a flawless performance. I was leery of Head because of his history with Paul Rosenberg. They were former college roommates and also were in a group together in the past.

Living on a bus with a bunch of hard-legged men was rough, being a married man and seeing these men with all these groupies. Groupies were waiting at the hotel at nearly every venue. Slim's road manager at the time, DT, basically was an asshole; his personality was shitty. Nobody really wanted to deal with him. I think Paul and Slim put up with him for as long as they did because they felt sorry for him because he had cancer the year before. He treated the fans like shit and fucked with our food. When no one was around, he would throw away the food because he wanted all of us to be vegetarians. He wanted to call all the shots, and it was bothering people.

At that time, we were doing an off-the-hook show in Pittsburgh. "The Crows" was like half hicks, half ravers, and a few thugs.A few people tried to rush the stage. At least the stage dives decreased to about three times. As usual, before and after the show Slim was drinking Bacardi and beer like a fish. After the show, everyone was chilling backstage. I let the finest girls backstage because it seemed like no one in the camp had any game. We let this one guy in who was like the ultimate Slim fan.We noticed him in the crowd because he had a mushroom tattooed on top of his head with "Slim Shady" written around it. He wanted to get back and party with Slim. He was begging, and Slim said, "OK, let him in." I warned him not to start any shit, because normally we only let girls in. About ten minutes later, I saw this dude whispering in Slim's ear so I went over there. He says to Slim, "Dude, I wanna snakebite you."We were like, "What the fuck is he talking about; what is that?" What he was saying was that he wanted to suck Slim's dick, so we embarrassed the shit out of him. He was begging to suck Slim's dick in the dressing room. Slim freaked out because he is homophobic as it is. We put all the guys out of the dressing room. We laughed about it later, but it was kind of scary because Slim started seeing some of the things he said in his songs come to pass.

April 13th

We were all bonding a little more at this time. The bus was really getting rough.We checked into hotels along the way in order to rest. I was a twenty-four-hour worker, the first one to get up and the last one to go to bed. I didn't have a life on the road at all. People think security is a glamorous job, but it isn't. I had to create my own fun and didn't realize how much fun I wasn't going to be having.We were now in Boston, probably one of the places where we were the least wanted. We had protesters there, and the first thing I suggested was not going into the dressing room until it was time for us to go on, in order to avoid trouble.We did the show and left, and everything went OK, even though they were really protesting Slim's lyrics.We did a radio show there, too, but there was some obvious hating going on anyway. Folks were there because it was free, not because they appreciated the craft. The show performance was dry because the crowd was dry.

Our next stop was New York, and I was nervous because of all the negative shit I had heard. The New York crowd was rough because they didn't get what they wanted. The dressing room was out of control because Paul and his partner kept bringing all their boys in the dressing room. One person from Vibe was trying to dog his way into the dressing room when Slim didn't want to see any press. Next thing I know, I see a negative write-up in the magazine; I guess he was trying to dog me out for being so big.The show was off the hook. Slim was drunk and high

Two beauties with Slim at Club Shine, NYC.

and was doing some crazy shit. He had me busting my ass. He was so fucked up, I thought he was going to OD. He decided he really wanted to give it to the crowd. He climbed up about fifteen feet to the top speaker and jumped down into the crowd. The crowd went nuts, and it was like a damn swimming pool. I was thinking, How the fuck am I going to get him from the middle of the crowd? I proceeded to dive in, like Moses parting the Red Sea, and landed at the bottom and grabbed Slim. People were grabbing his shirt and pulling at his pants. On our way back to the stage, they started doing the same to me, and I was just beating people off of us. At that point, I knew that he was trying to test me to see just how much I had his back. I knew he was going to have me working. Later that night, we went to Club Shine in downtown NYC. Slim had continued drinking heavily at Shine and became paranoid about some Latino dudes staring him down. Of course, Slim took it as a threat and confronted the guys and was cursing at them. The next thing I knew, Slim had swung on one of the three guys. I immediately pushed the dudes back and grabbed Slim and carried him out the side door to the limo. After putting him in the limo where he was safe, the promoter of

Club Shine and I had an altercation. The promoter was demanding that Slim come back into the club. When I told him no, he was pissed. At that point, I was done talking and ready to whip some ass! The promoter was very disrespectful. While the promoter continued to blah, blah, I ate my fully lit Cuban cigar. That was enough for the promoter to back the fuck up and say, "Fuck it!" We then left to prepare for the next day.

That Friday, we did another show, and at this one nothing special happened. That day Slim had no time to sleep and couldn't sober up due to press conferences. He took drugs to stay up and to fall asleep. He was dependent on chemicals, I guess from the pressure of the shows and the press. I think the drugs came in mostly because of DT (his first road manager). DT would always pull Slim aside with his knapsack and give him drugs. Slim would take Ecstasy and shrooms before every show, and DT always furnished them. He would always try to slip someone something, and you had to watch him because he would try to slip something into your drink or food when you weren't looking. I told him if I ever suspected him of fucking with my shit, I was going to kick his ass. I attribute Slim's excessive use of drugs to DT. Although Slim was a grown man and could make his own decisions, DT was extremely influential. I saw Slim cry for the first time in Boston when couldn't deal with the pressure of the tour. He broke down, and it was a sad sight. They were pressuring him for more press and more interviews, and it drove him crazy that they were always asking him the same questions. He cried and stormed out of the hotel, and Proof went after him to console him. He missed Hailey, his daughter, and I saw him as human because of that. That was the first time I ever thought of him other than as an entertainer. He was real—and had real feelings—even though he was intoxicated all the time.

On April 17th, we headed to California for the first time. We rode on a private jet about the size of a Pinto, and it fit me like a pair of pants from the eighth grade. We had to go through Customs, and Slim had a pocketful of drugs, so he started stuffing pills inside sandwiches. I couldn't believe it! I knew I wasn't holding shit for anybody. I thought Customs was going to bring out the dogs, but they didn't. I saw at that point that Slim didn't care about anyone else's comfort—nothing outside of his own world matters, and he's very self-centered.

We arrived in LA just after an earthquake hit. We went to a hotel right on the beach. It was a real nice hotel, with an oceanfront view, just like in the movies. The toilets were heated and everything. We were in California for three days shooting the video for "Role Model," and it was a long-ass shoot. It was on this shoot that I met Sarge and Rowe. They were Dre's security. They watched me like a hawk, despite the fact that I

The crew: Byron, Slim, DJ Head, MC Proof, and Paul Rosenberg (Slim's manager).

was working for Slim. That made me nervous. They thought that opposing forces had sent me to infiltrate the aftermath. We all laugh about that to this day. The shooting lasted for sixteen, eighteen and, sometimes twenty hours over three days. Slim had to do his own stunts, which put him under a lot of stress. I took care of him, but I still wasn't getting any type of response or respect. He hadn't opened up to me. He would just take off sometimes without me. He would lie about his whereabouts and didn't grasp the fact that he was a well-known star now and needed security. He thought he could handle himself, and I had to talk to him about trying to shake me all the time and that I was hired to protect him. The video shoot started to go more smoothly after that. One time, his road manager disappeared for a while, and I had to step in and take over that responsibility. I didn't get any thanks for that either, even though I did go out of my way and above my duties. It was cool seeing Dre and Slim work side by side. His wife and kid accompanied Dre, and they by his side while he worked. It reminded me of my family. Slim started getting sick, and things were getting hectic, but finally the shoot ended and

Slim and D-12 in Detroit outside "The Shelter"

everyone could get some rest.

There was tension because Paul and DT were at odds since DT went missing in action at the video shoot. DT treated the fans like shit for real then, and he lagged behind when we wereloading the bus, which put Slim's life in jeopardy. Plus he took Slim out to sign autographs without me, and I checked him about that. He wasn't hearing anything I had to say, so that became our first run-in.

April 28th, Austin, Texas

This was the wildest, most diverse crowd I had ever seen. They were off the hook! There were at least 3,000 people there—the rowdiest people I had seen in my life—but all of the different ethnic groups were in harmony. They were fighting to get to Slim. They were rushing the stage and throwing shit. They twisted up the bicycle barricade and threw it like it was a pretzel. People were building human ladders and rushing the stage like that. I had to put Slim on my shoulders and run him to the dressing room with a wall of security guys around me. Someone pissed everybody off by throwing a beer bottle through the dressing room window. It was wild!

On May 5th, we did Vegas. I was stressed out, tired, and missing my family. Living out of a suitcase and living on buses was getting tiring. The show was funny because some kid wore an ICP T-shirt to the concert. Why would this kid wear an ICP T-shirt to a Slim Shady concert? Everyone knows that Slim hates ICP. So, upon Slim's instructions, the crowd ripped the T-shirt off the guy and beat his ass and threw him out of the concert. After the show, the guy was waiting at the bus in another ICP T-shirt, saying he wanted to talk to Slim, but I think he wanted to do something to Slim, to be honest. Slim said he wanted to go talk to the kid, but I knew he was going to go over there and beat the kid up so I didn't let him. Next thing I knew, Gus (the tour manager) said he got a call from MGM security saying that a fifteen-year-old girl was missing who said she was coming to the concert and asked if we'd seen her. We said "no" and shrugged it off. That night the police called my room, and I told them we didn't have any fifteen-year-old girls with us and got off the phone. The instant I hung up, they were knocking at our doors, searching our rooms. I told everyone we needed to leave because obviously they were trying to pin something on us—and since this was Vegas anything could happen. We got the hell out of there!

May 8th, Los Angeles, California

It was crazy that night! All of these people were in the VIP room—Slim's people and Dre and his people—and my job was difficult, but Sarge and Rowe helped me out a lot.We kept getting a request from inhouse security for this fighter, Tank Abbots, to come up and meet Slim— he was demanding to meet Slim.The name sounded familiar, but we weren't letting anybody else up in the room.We proceeded to do the show, and the electricity of that show was amazing! Slim had a chance to meet Dustin Hoffman earlier, and he convinced him to be the mummy as a stage prop that night. No one in the crowd knew that Dustin Hoffman was the mummy, and Dre did a surprise spot and performed "G Thing," as well. It was off the hook! Suddenly, we noticed the crowd part and these three goons making their way to the front. I knew then why the name Tank Abbots sounded familiar to me. He was one of the "Toughman" champions WCW-type muthafuckas. He and I were talking shit back and forth, and I knew that I had backup from Dre's security, as well. DT busted Tank Abbots over the head with a bottle, and basically we were fighting him offstage for the whole concert.We found out that they came looking for us at the hotel that night, too, and we told hotel security about the earlier altercation and not to let those guys in. It was wild!

On May 9, 1999, there was a hip-hop riot, and guess who started it? Slim Shady, of course! We were in San Francisco, California, at The Fillmore when it happened. Slim was in the middle of a hype performance when a hater started heckling him. Slim took notice of the guy and retaliated by dissing him. The heckler continued, and Slim got pissed. The next thing I knew, Slim had jumped off the stage with a flying right cross. Unfortunately, he hit the wrong guy, and then it was on! The crowd swallowed Slim like a giant mouth, and I proceeded in after him. Slim was getting his ass whipped by the same people that helped him sell triple platinum! When I waded into the furious crowd, I was punched. I then turned to the SOB that struck me and beat him into bloody unconsciousness. I had forgotten all about Slim. I had beaten this guy until he was out cold. The crowd could no longer support his weak legs. Immediately, pandemonium broke out.There were more people fighting in the crowd. DJ Head jumped in to fight; Billy, the soundman, left the booth to scrap; the Interscope street team was throwing blows; and The Beatnuts were kicking some ass. Young Z from the Outsidaz and I were back-to-back knocking muthafuckas out! Finally, I noticed Slim on the bottom of a shit-kicking pile with this big fella on top of him. Proof and I started whaling on this idiot. Proof kicked the

This groupie wanted more than Slim's autograph (NYC).

guy in the head a few times, and I gave this dude some nice rib shots he won't ever forget. Finally, we picked Slim up and threw him back on the stage. We all had to fight to get to safety because the crowd had turned against us. I rushed Slim to the side of the stage and told Gus that we needed to get the fuck out of there! Gus said, "The show must go on, or they're going to kill our ass!" and we all reluctantly agreed. We attempted to brush it off as the crowd shouted, "FUCK YOU, SLIM! FUCK YOU, SLIM!" Proof came to the rescue by grabbing the mic and hyping the crowd to another level. He said, "Ya'll muthafuckas like that shit!" They screamed, "HELL, YEAH!" Proof stood side by side with George Clinton of the P-Funk Allstars. He continued by telling the crowd that Detroit muthafuckas whoop ass! The crowd went nuts. DJ Head ripped the turntables with some hype mixing and scratching. When Slim came back onstage the crowd showed genuine love like the riot never happened. Slim made the crowd go into overdrive by performing "Still Don't Give A Fuck!" The energy was unbelievable. Everywhere you looked, fans were crowd surfing and moshing in the pit. It was amazing to see a fickle crowd cause chaos then release love for Slim. Slim gave

MC Proof saves the show once again in Texas.

the crowd two ovations that night, and they deserved it! After the show, a satisfied crowd mobbed us. Some groupies actually thought that the big brawl was part of the show. We told them that we always do that! That next day we awoke with bumps, bruises, and scratches from the unforgettable riot.

Sunday, May 16th, Minneapolis, Minnesota

The show was off the hook, and the crowd was feeling us. We had the super groupie at this show. During the autograph session at this show in the main lobby, she got down on her knees in front of everybody and tried to suck Slim's dick. She unzipped his pants and everything, but he wouldn't let her. Rumor has it that some of the guys from the opening acts took her back to the hotel and got her drunk and, from what I understand, ran bustos on her while she was unconscious and left her in her own vomit. When she came to, she was ready to fight and

Slim is high and DT takes the credit.

call the police, but they somehow convinced her not to. I know she was a freak, but no one deserves to be taken advantage of like that. The most tripped out part about it is that somehow the soundman, Billy, hooked up with her and ended up falling in love with her. She was the same freak everybody ran through. He even brought her on tour with us. Everybody was freaking out that Billy chose to turn a ho into a housewife, but that was his thing. To make a long story short, Billy married her. And she was still trying to fuck and suck on the whole crew!

Monday, May 17th, Lawrence, Kansas

On this day and in this city and state, I didn't expect to see anything I saw. First of all, Slim's mother lives in Kansas with her family. Slim and his mom actually communicating was something to see. I told him up front that I wouldn't get involved in any domestic shit. I wasn't going to throw her off the bus or anything like that, no matter what she did, because that was his mom. So his mom and a lot of other relatives showed up, not because they were happy to see him but because they all wanted something from him. Gus booked us in this hotel that was old and had a plantation feel to it. The room I was in had these doors that would keep opening all the way back up even though I would keep shutting them. I would hear knocks at the door, and no one would ever be there, and that shit was eerie to me. When the crew and I kicked it, we found that we all had been experiencing the same problems. When we asked the lady at the front desk for directions to the post office, we told her what was happening. She was surprised that we didn't know this hotel was haunted, and she proceeded to show us pictures in a photo album—all having this ghastly image of half a man or a man with no head in the background. We were all freaked out by that but weren't too worried, mostly because everyone was going to be tore down that night anyway.

Before the show, Slim was getting high and drunk on the tour bus, as usual. Everyone was enjoying himself or herself listening to Tupac, which was a ritual. The fun began when Slim's twenty relatives came to the bus. We kicked the groupies off the bus to make room for his family, who were all drunk as hell. I guess the apple doesn't fall too far from the tree. It was like "South Park" mixed with "The Beverly Hillbillies." I met his mom, who was like eighty pounds soaking wet with boots on. She appeared to be a nice lady, but she brought a photographer with her and charged people $20 to take pictures with her son and sold pictures to the local news for future stories. Slim told me not to let his mom onstage with him because she would surely try to become part of the show. I put DT on that job, and the show went over well. On the tour bus afterward, Slim and his relatives reminisced—with minor altercations—until he had them leave so that he could have some real fun.

I never saw so many free-spirited groupies who were willing to do whatever you asked them before in my life. I never saw so many young lesbians together all at one time, either. These three girls, two blond and one mixed black and Indian, showed up at the tour bus saying how they wanted to fulfill a fantasy of all three of them by sleeping with Slim. And they were hot, too. I told Slim about the proposition, and he said that he was with it, so I took the girls up to the hotel room, and the age-old thing happened—a call from the girlfriend back home. Slim's then-girlfriend, Kim Scott, called him, and they went through their usual argument rituals—he hung up on her, she hung up on him, etc. I situated the girls, who got buck-naked and start sucking one another's juicy breasts and rubbing one another's clitoris'. The ladies were getting busy on the bed while Slim was in the bathroom arguing with Kim. I had my camera ready because that's all the fun I was allowed to have. I kept the photos on file for any future court dates or false accusations of rape. I was still trying to hurry Slim out of the bathroom. The girls were eating one another out and were getting wetter by the minute. They were anxious and impatient waiting on Slim. One girl screamed in hot orgasmic pleasure, as her friend tantalized her hole with her tongue, "Oooh, Oooh! Where is Slim?" I rushed to get Slim again, and suddenly he said he wasn't doing it! I went out to try to delay the ladies. I said, "Slim's going to be longer than expected, but there are some other fellas who would gladly keep you company meanwhile."

These girls totally ignored me in the midst of their smorgasbord. Their whole mind set was about having sex with Slim. I was frustrated because I couldn't do anything. Slim was in the bathroom on the phone arguing with Kim. The rest of the fellas were mad because the girls they were with weren't putting out. I told the girls, "Slim won't be boning you this evening, due to some unforeseen circumstances. But the DJ and a couple of the other guys want to break you off a little something." Slim basically could have delegated an orgy that night, but Kim stole his mojo! I gave the ladies Slim's message, "Ladies, hook up with my boys, and I'll try to get with y'all a little later." I said, "Ain't no use in being stingy with it." The ladies were like, "Naw, fuck that! We just wanna get with Slim. You got us up here!" and I was like, "No, I didn't force y'all up here. You came up here by your own choice. Ladies, you decided to get butt-ass naked and start eating one another out. Therefore, if y'all ain't fuckin, y'all got to go!" They were like, "Just like that?" I said, "Yeah, just like that!" The ladies said, "Well, it ain't that kind of party." "So then! Well, your clothes are out in the hallway, then!" and I kicked them out. Everybody was like, "Damn, Naz, why you do that?" and I said, "Look, they wanted to get with Slim! They couldn't get with Slim. They didn't want to get with any of the fellas. So, I just diffused the problem right there. They had to go. We avoid things escalating and them possibly yelling rape at some point, so I nipped the problem in the bud." Unfortunately, not everyone saw it like that, but oh well.

But the night was still young. By this time, most everyone was passed out from being drunk, and I was sober, as usual, so I decided to go down to the bus to get a brew. There was another party going on in the bus. The bus driver was there and a bunch of college girls and their boyfriends, and once again the girls were getting busy with one another. I was like, damn, there must be something in the air tonight! As usual, I had my camera—the only fun I got to have—and I was like, "Yo, can I get some pictures for my scrapbook?" That was one of the reasons, but another reason was in case someone tried to holler rape, I would

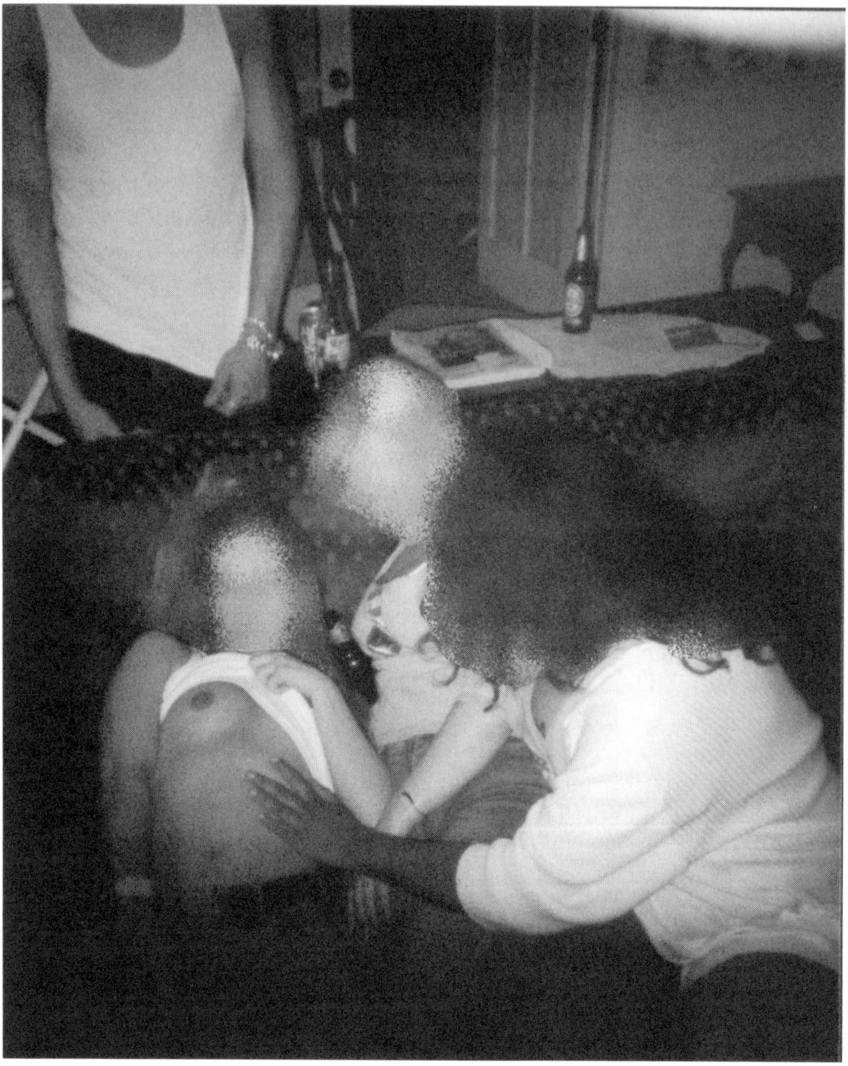

The Kansas State threesome that wanted to sleep with Slim.

have pictures of them doing voluntary sexual acts. So I got pictures of them flashing one another, showing their body piercings and tattoos, and basically just demeaning themselves. One girl got feisty and started feeling on her girlfriend's breasts while they were dancing. Everybody was drunk, and this one guy decided he wanted to get freaky with someone other than his girlfriend, and his girlfriend was like, "That's fucked up, but it's cool." So then she tells me and G (the bus driver) that she wants to show us something, so she leads us to the rear. We were wondering what the hell she was going to show us, so I had my camera ready. So she bends over and shows us this tattoo on her ass, she shows us her nipple rings, and she pulls off her Daisy Duke shorts and gets in the spread-eagle position and shows us her clitoris ring. Of course, every position was a Kodak moment for me. It was a beautiful clitoris ring, needless to say. I took it upon myself to leave at that time because things were getting out of hand. I was reaching the point of temptation that I didn't want to get too close to, so I went ahead and retired for the night. So, if you're ever in Lawrence, Kansas, and you're looking for some young ladies, go to the university there. There's only one university, and that's where the action is.

May 19th, Milwaukee, Wisconsin (Club Rain)

Nothing major happened that night as far as the show. However, that night I learned much about the people around me, as well as myself. I was eager that night because the next day I was going home to spend a few days with my wife and my kids. It felt good to be close geographically to Michigan, and I was looking forward to going home. We were loading the bus and, as I told you before, DT, Eminem's road manager, and I were always at odds. Our conflict was mainly due to putting Eminem's safety at risk. That night, we left Wisconsin to go to DC, and DT had left his tour book behind without realizing it. Proof, Eminem's hype man and a friend of mine, told me that DT had written some negative things in that book about me. He was taking notes about anything anyone did that he found negative, and he had a lot of negative things written about everyone in that book. He kept it as "evidence" of how everyone else was incompetent, so that he could gain Slim's confidence so that Slim would give him comanagement. It justified a lot of his previous actions of undermining Paul and a lot of other people. I didn't turn the book in to Paul because I didn't want to appear as though I was trying to spill the beans on DT because that seemed petty to me. Proof and I were the only ones who knew what was in that book. All I did was gather the information that I needed and make a mental note of it. From that point on, I watched DT because I knew he was the conniving son of a bitch I always thought he was. Later on, DT's true colors showed themselves, and the other guys saw that I was right about him in the first place. At one point, Paul came and asked me how I felt about DT. Since they were firing DT, I told him that I had read the negative things DT wrote about him, me, and a lot of other people, and that if we weren't going to work as a team I couldn't be comfortable under those circumstances because I knew I was doing my job. That was probably the only time Paul and I were on the same page and ever really communicated with each other.

May 20th

Home, sweet home, and it felt good. I got to play with the kids and see the wife, but little did I know that the 21st would be a day of drama. I thought a simple trip to Grand Rapids would go smoothly, but I was wrong. It was cool because I drove my own car to the venue rather than ride with the rest of them. Slim did one of the dumbest things ever: he had one of his mistresses stay with him an extra day. Now, everyone knows a real playa wouldn't play it that close. He was only two hours away from home, in his home state, and he wanted to have one of his mistresses stay with him, knowing how crazy Kim was! He underestimated Kim. Kim told him she didn't want to come to Grand Rapids, so he decided to have his mistress,Kessia, a young lady from Florida, stay an extra day with him. She was cool, and we regarded her as more than just a groupie, and she was definitely more mentally stable than Kim. Of course, the first thing I noticed was the mistake Slim made by still having Kessia there. Everyone was trying to convince him to get rid of Kessia in case Kim changed her mind and decided to come to Grand Rapids, which is exactly what happened. So we had to hurry up and get Kessia on the first flight out, and she understood because she knew about Kim, while, of course, Kim didn't know about her. Now the whole crew was on lie patrol just in case Slim got caught up, which I didn't like at all because Kim raises hell as it is anyway since she hates the fact that Slim is always on the road. She hates the fact that he has groupies, and she really doesn't know how to deal with Slim's success. So Kim checked into the room, and the first thing she noticed was a message for Slim on his phone. So, her being his girlfriend and all, she decided to play the message. As luck would have it, it was a lovey-dovey message from Kessia, saying how she misses him and can't wait to come see him again, etc. So Kim got pissed. I mean she went through the roof! We got hip to her finding out ahead of time by the crew manager while we were at a sound check. So Slim started the lie, and we all put our heads together to come up with a lie that would keep Kessia out of it as much as possible, since she was such a nice girl. The lie we came up with was that Kessia was a stalker who was madly in love with Slim, and she called every hotel and would say and do anything to get to him. When we got back to the hotel, we saw Kim sitting at the bar, letting some guy push up on her. The first thing out of her mouth was, "What the fuck is some bitch doing on your answering machine, Marshall, and you know about it!" So, we all were like, "What? Oh, that's Amy, the stalker bitch." I'm telling you, that day we all lied so good, it became the truth to us. I mean we all should have won Oscars for our acting jobs. However, Kim wasn't really buying it, so I pulled her aside and did a little extra bullshitting to convince her, saying that even though she dogs Slim out he would never do anything to jeopardize what they have because he loves her, blah, blah, blah. This was one of the few times they kissed and made up, even though she threw it in his face a few times throughout the day. Somehow we made it through that one. Lying for Slim just doesn't always pay off.

A few days passed on the tour. We did Detroit and Cincinnati. It was May 27th, and I was beginning to come to grips with how I felt about Slim, Shady Tours, and Paul Rosenberg. We arrived in Atlanta and did the most hype show we had encountered at that point. There was a sold-out mixed crowd, and the show was off the hook. That night was wild and unforgettable because it affected me mentally, physically, and spiritually. It was a downslide for me, and it showed me that I was a security guard and nothing else—which means people don't look at you as human, don't care about your family, and don't look at you as an emotional being.

On this night, the show was wild, and it was off the hook. Slim was rocking the crowd. They were amped. He would jump off the stage and slap hands with the crowd or crowd surf, and I was always right behind him whenever he did that. I noticed this one guy in particular on the balcony who would jump down from the balcony onto the stage and act a fool whenever Slim would jump into the crowd, but by the time we got back onstage he would jump back into the crowd, so we couldn't catch him. He did this at least two more times. Then the guy decided to rush the stage while Slim and I were on it. He was a big guy, about 6'2", 250 pounds, and he was obviously high. He jumped from the balcony to the speaker to the stage and started rushing full speed at Slim, and he didn't look like he wanted to give him a hug, either. I positioned myself between him and Slim, and the guy sped up like he wanted to buck me like a football player, so I stepped out of his way as he charged forward and nailed him as he went past me. I mean, I knocked the shit out of this guy. He flew off the stage and hit the barricade to the stage. I knew I knocked him out, and if I didn't, the fall should have done it. But that

The Kansas State trio that wanted to sleep with Slim.

wasn't the case. This guy was high on something, I don't know what. He just sat there a few seconds and shook it off and proceeded to try to get back onstage. I tried to signal the five security guys who were on crowd control to get this guy out of there, but they were afraid of him; they didn't want to work, they were just there to get the money. So I jumped down and grabbed the guy, but he kept trying to get away from me, and I started punching him in the back of his head over and over. Finally, his legs buckled, and before he hit the ground, I got him in a hold where he couldn't move his arms and started to escort him out the side door where the police were. Now the five crowd control guys decided they wanted to help. They rushed over and grabbed me and the guy which caused us all to fall. In the process of trying to break my fall, I dislocated my shoulder. The pain was excruciating, but I still couldn't let the guy go because I knew I was vulnerable at that point; these five security guys wouldn't have my back. I managed to escort the guy out with my one good arm, and I really cursed those security guys out, probably more from the pain I was in than the fact that they wouldn't help me, even though that pissed me off, too. By this time the show was over, and we got on the bus, and I was in so much pain that I couldn't even trip out.

My armpit socket was hanging down by my pecs. Slim was shitting bricks. He was running around like a chicken with his head cut off. He kept saying, "Is there anything you need? Here, take a shot!" So, I took a few shots of Bacardi light, and I damn near finished the bottle by the time the ambulance arrived. Slim was real apologetic and thankful because he didn't know what was going on. He made a lot of promises, like taking care of my hospital bills and saying that he would get me anything I needed. They turned out to be empty promises, but they sounded good at the time. I thought I would be at the hospital alone, but, much to my surprise, DT, of all people, came with me. I wonder what his real motivation was in coming with me, whether he enjoyed seeing me in pain, or why it took me being in pain for him to be nice to me. Anyway, I wasn't worried while at the emergency room, thinking that since I was Slim Shady's bodyguard they would take care of me. The doctor, a young guy about thirty-three years of age, told me that from the X-rays I was lucky that I hadn't broken my collar bone, and if I had any less muscle mass I probably would have. He told me that they were going to give me a shot of morphine and then pop my shoulder back into place. It took some time for the doctor to convince me that I wouldn't feel any pain, and even after he gave me the shot, I still tried to protest, but I was out of it before I could even finish my sentence. From what I was told, it took three doctors to pop my shoulder back into its socket, and DT also told me that when it popped back in, it made this resounding popping sound, and I came out of it, sat up, screamed my head off, and then fell back into unconsciousness. They gave me some smelling salts and another shot to bring me back to, and the first thing I said was, "Y'all got anything to eat around here?" Everybody got a kick out of that. I was in pain for about a month and had to wear my arm in a sling and take Vicodin. Slim got a big kick out of me taking Vicodin because that was one of his favorite drugs. Besides, he figured with me being on Vicodin, he could get a few free pills here and there. That time off was a period of transition for me. I learned a lot about myself and realized what I was putting at risk. I was jeopardizing my life and my health for a man whom I really knew nothing about. I got into this security thing just to get in a better position to get my own label off the ground. I quickly realized that I needed to be getting something more out of it. I wasn't even making that much money. It wasn't worth the risk.

I looked at the situation more deeply because I didn't expect to get hurt on the job; it just wasn't an aspect I had considered. So I began to feel depressed, used, and neglected because no one really had much to

Byron and Dean (Slim's A&R man) outside the shoot for "Guilty Conscience"

say to me about it except periodically asking me if it hurt or not, but I could tell no one really cared for the most part. The biggest topic was, "How long is it going to take for you to heal?" and I was like, "Damn, it just happened. It's going take a couple of months," and that it did. This happened during the first part of the Slim Shady tour, and at home I was getting a lot of stares and people were like, "Damn, how are you going to protect Slim while you're hurt?" I was like, "Well, right now I can't." I had to get some other people to cover me. I felt thrown away and unappreciated. I saw where I stood with Shady Tours. At this point in time, I didn't have a contract with Shady Tours. The contract was getting paid. I still believed the empty promise that my doctor bills would be taken care of. I couldn't go back to work at GM with my shoulder in a sling because it would cause too many questions to be asked about my injury. I was on leave for something else. Besides, I was working for Shady Tours when I got hurt. They should have been taking care of me while I was on leave. However, Shady Tours' response to that was,"Well, we're going to give you $350 a week workman's comp."That couldn't pay the bills! And it took them two months to give me that. That was some bullshit! I was thinking about my wife and family. I had some money put aside, but I wasn't planning on spending that. I was counting on them to take care of me until we went back on the road. I see. I'm good enough to go out there and work and get hurt, but I am not good enough for you to look out for while I am hurt. At that point I realized that I would have to get a contract or something a little more concrete if I was going to continue working for Slim. My wife was a little upset because she had to change her lifestyle, and I couldn't really pick up our baby boy because of my shoulder. I started weighing out the odds, with me getting hurt and not receiving adequate compensation while I was off, so I asked them to at least give me an advance toward the next tour. They agreed to do that, but that meant the next tour I was basically working for free. You would think that they would have at least considered the fact that I took a leave of absence from my job to work for them, but that meant nothing to them. They didn't give a fuck as long as they benefited from it. This was a turning point where the business relationship turned bitter, because I got wiser and I began to see where we were headed together, and it wasn't in a positive direction.

2

WARPED TOURS

Well, it was the Fourth of July, and we headed out on the Warped Tour with my shoulder operating at about 70 percent of its normal performance. The Warped Tour was supposed to be an easy tour, and it was for the most part. I was going through therapy for my shoulder, and the tour was only scheduled for five weeks, anyway. The purpose of my going was that I had taken out an advance on my pay. I basically worked the first two weeks for free because I was paying back the money that I borrowed since I had no income while I was off for my injury. By this time, Slim's promises to take care of me that he made while I was in the ambulance had proven to be false. He left all the financial decisions up to his manager, Paul, who he knew wasn't taking care of me, but he did nothing about it. The only thing they did was call me once a week to see if I would be ready to go on the road for the next tour. I told them I was going through therapy and had a pretty bad tear in my muscle tissue, and all I could do was heal one day at a time. Their main concern wasn't if I needed anything or any money, it was whether or not I would be ready to go on tour. I can say that this was a learning process for me, and I learned from my mistakes.

The Warped Tour was more alternative than anything else, so I didn't have to deal with a lot of the crazed groupies like before. With my job being pretty much laid back at this point, it allowed me a lot of time to do some soul searching, as I had done while I was off injured. It wasn't easy for me to do, but I detached myself from Slim Shady and his manager on a personal level. It was hard because we worked together day and night, but it had to be done. I passed my time talking to Proof and DJ Head and calling home to my wife, which resulted in a high phone bill. On this tour, I was able to learn that I was definitely underpaid. We had a chance to mix and mingle with the crews from the other headlining acts, and we were all kicking around some figures on what we were getting paid and found out that we were all making less than our counterparts who worked for other acts who were, ironically, less successful than Slim Shady was.We felt like fools in the eyes of our peers because they were like, "Damn, we haven't sold a third as many records as you guys have, and we make more than you do!" I always felt that I should have been getting more than $1200 a week, but it all happened so fast in the beginning, I didn't get a chance to ever renegotiate my pay. Every time I would bring it to the attention of Paul Rosenberg, he would always promise that we would talk about it at another time. Some of us felt that Slim had nothing to do with it, but we came to find out he was the one who gave the final approval of everyone's pay. Slim would always try to act like he didn't know and blamed it on Paul and his accountants, but realistically they didn't make a move without his approval. They would try to be a friend in your face but fuck you financially. The "friend" tactic worked with some of these guys on the tour because they had grown up with Slim and Paul, and Slim played on that when it came time to paying them unsubstantially, but that didn't work for me.

Slim made more money than every act on that tour, so there was no excuse. There were people who left their jobs or took leaves from their jobs to work for Slim. DJ Head gave a fine performance every time he spun those records to keep the crowd hype. Proof put together Slim's show as far as the ideas and the order of the songs, but did he get paid what he was worth? No, he didn't. I didn't. DJ Head didn't. I hate to say this, but none of the brothers made equal pay. Slim is always talking about how he hates racism, but he and Paul Rosenberg were the main ones keeping us financially unequal. The soundman, Billy, made damn good money, and he only worked like an hour a day. He made at least $1,500 a week. Gus Brandt, whom I consider to be a good friend of mine because he gave me a lot of advice and information regarding the business, knew he was making less than he should be, but he accepted it because he figured that he could help Slim and Paul have a more successful tour with him being a part of it.We were all upset over our pay

Paul trying to scheme on getting Byron fired.

scale. It wasn't like the money wasn't there, because I knew for a fact that it was there. I knew what went down, when, and why it went down. I never deliberately looked for this information; it usually fell into my lap, with Slim being by my side most of the time. Even when he wasn't by my side, financial information fell into my lap.

On this particular tour, Slim was making $15,000 a day, which was like $75,000 a week. Over a five-week period, that was a nice bit of change. That's not even including his merchandising, which he never followed up on because he left that up to Paul. So, the money was definitely there. It hurt to find out that out of these other crews who worked for groups who hadn't even sold 200,000 records, their lowest-paid member made more money then we did, and they had bands so they definitely had more heads to pay. Slim continued to pretend like he didn't know what was going on, and Paul was content as long as he was making more than everyone else. It was sad. I determined that I made about $5 an hour working around the clock seven days a week for $1,200 a week. This only added to my frustration. I decided to draw up a proposal and present it to Paul because some changes definitely had to be made. I took some time and conferred with Gus, the tour manager, during this process, and he told me I was getting fucked with no Vaseline. He said that I should be making at least $1,500 but that most security guys were making two grand a week. He said that since I was a 24-hour man and that I did a lot of things that I shouldn't have to do, I should be making more than $1,200. He made that coming out of high school. He said "Byron, they're fucking you bad." Gus was making a lot of sense to me, and he had more experience in this business than everyone combined. He's worked with everybody from the Foo Fighters to the Stones, so he knows what he's talking about. Gus was not a greedy man. He was fair, and he wanted to see people treated fairly. He didn't start to open up until he realized that he was getting screwed out of his money. He took a pay cut in an effort to work with Paul and Slim and teach them about touring, but they took Gus' kindness for weakness, and Gus is not a weak man; he's very smart, very intelligent. Paul and Slim didn't realize that at any time Gus could have stolen all of Slim's money and ran, but he didn't—he stayed and did his job to the T. But did he ever get a "Thank you" or a "Good job, Gus"? Did he get a proper bonus, or even the proper pay? No, he didn't.

We were getting mistreated! So, I put together a proposal for Paul and Slim, asking them for life insurance in case of my death so my family would be taken care of. I knew that if they barely did anything for me while I was alive, they damn sure wouldn't do anything for my family in the event of my death. I asked to be paid $2,000 a week during workweeks and for a retainer of $1,200 a week when we weren't on tour. I asked for sick days. I am a businessman, and I like things to be done in writing. Contracts keep guidelines. I presented this proposal to Paul and Slim, and they were intimidated that I had my own personal CPA draw up this proposal. They didn't really know how to deal with it, or didn't want to deal with it. They went back and forth about it and procrastinated for about a month.

In New York, Paul and Slim called me into a meeting with them to resolve this issue. They told me they liked working with me and that they didn't want to lose me. At this time, I was up for a promotion at my job at GM to become shop chairman, where I could have made $100,000 a year easily, without the inconsistency. I was willing to stay on with Paul and Slim because I had my own label that I was trying to get off the ground. I was in a position to make a lot of connections in the music business, plus possibly draw the attention of Paul and Slim to my own groups.

Paul basically told me that what I was asking for was ridiculous. Was it ridiculous for me to ask for some sound security working for this man for whom I had left my job, my wife and kids, my home for, whom I was jeopardizing my health and my life for? I was being told that it was ridiculous for me to ask for some security. He shut down on the idea of a written contract—he didn't want a contract. I asked him why it was OK for him to have a written contract with Slim Shady, but I couldn't have a written contract ensuring that they wouldn't move me out at the last minute when I jeopardized a stable, good-paying job to work for them. Was it ridiculous for me to ask for a stable environment, for life insurance, for ample pay for me to meet my financial goals? I sacrificed a lot. I couldn't convince him to see that, or maybe he was threatened by the fact that I had knowledge of self and the industry and I was close to Slim, so therefore in his eyes I posed a possible threat to his job. He knew that I knew how he operated, as well. I tried to convey the message to him that I was there to do security, not to try to steal Slim Shady, but he didn't understand that.

The thing that drove me the most crazy was the way that Slim played possum, acting like he didn't know what was going on when the whole time behind the scenes he called all the shots. An issue would be brought to Paul, he would take it to Slim, and Slim would tell him how he wanted it to be handled, and Paul would handle it. Afterward, Slim would play dumb. For a long time, I honestly believed that Slim was in the dark about these issues because he was always drunk or high or dealing with his marital and family problems. Over time, I realized from the way things progressed that Slim was very much aware and responsible for the way things were handled. I don't entirely blame Paul for the way things were, but he definitely had a way of getting into Slim's head and influencing his decisions. Paul was the evil, conniving one in the picture, but Slim couldn't see that because he couldn't think for himself. Everyone around him thought for Slim Shady because he couldn't think for himself. That's what we were paid to do. Proof thought of the show format; DJ Head thought of the beats; I thought of ways to keep him safe and thought up lies for him.We all did things we didn't have to do for him, and none of us were getting compensated adequately for our efforts.

They didn't even try to honor my proposal. They didn't even try to meet me halfway. Realistically, I knew that they weren't going to give me $2,000 a week, but I figured I would at least shoot high and maybe they'd give me at least half of what I asked for. But all I got was an extra $100 a week on the basis that they were saving for Slim's retirement. I said, "You know what? That's great that you and his accountants are concerned about Slim's future, because most managers and accountants aren't concerned with their artists' retirement, so that's great that you care about him. But don't forget about all the people who work for him and contribute to his success, because we have mouths to feed, as well.We have futures." I even proposed a 401K or an annuity program, but they shot that down, as well. I can't say that right away I saw that there was racial dissension among the Shady camp, because the camp members were very diverse. There were Jews, whites, blacks, a Mexican, and a German, to say the least, but I can say one thing that has not changed is the fact that the brothers were paid less. I call that oppression, and that oppression comes through Paul, and Slim agrees to it, even though he acts like he doesn't know what's going on, and that's the sad part.

So, with my new $100 extra a week, I realized that I was making $185 a day, less than what I could have been making back home at GM on straight time alone. Again I tolerated this in the hope of making connections and gathering resources that would enable me to get my own label, Big Willz Recordz, with my group, the Wadsquad, off the ground. At the end of July and at the beginning of September in California, I realized that there were a lot of paper gangsters in this business.They couldn't do shit to you physically, but they could beat you down on paper. That's what Paul and Slim were: paper gangsters. I knew they couldn't do shit to me physically, but behind closed doors on paper, where they called all the shots, what could I do? They killed me on paper. I continued, though, because I figured I could gain some things that money couldn't buy: networking and connections.

In my downtime, I presented them with packages, and I knew we had some good stuff, but they always found ways to hate on it. I even presented some packages to Paul to possibly submit for some soundtracks, but he never even listened to them. I knew then that it was time for me to make some things happen for myself. Slim would sleep in until like 2:00 p.m. while we were out in California recording his album, and I would spend my free mornings taking cabs to this radio station or that radio station, as well as various record companies. I got a few connections, but it was reinforced to me that unless you had a referral or were talking to the man who made the big decision, you weren't going to get anywhere. That put a damper on things for the moment. I decided to make the best of my time while in LA, so I spent some time with Sarge and Rowe, Dre's security, who schooled me on how to adjust to the California lifestyle. They told me about how people at Death Row can cause problems, as well as some other people. After being in California for about two weeks, I decided to get certified, to get my executive protection order as well as a few CCW permits. I did this to make myself more well-rounded and hoped that by taking my status to a more pro-

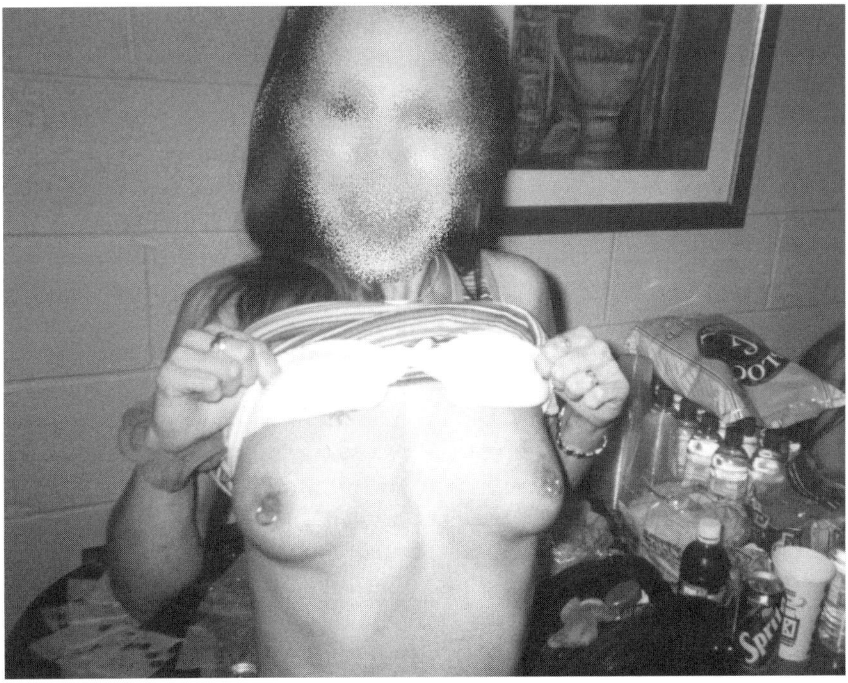

Nice eyes! Arizona Warped Tour.

fessional level, I would get more adequate pay from Slim and Paul. I also made myself more marketable, in case I wanted to do other forms of security or security for other artists. I took all my classes in the mornings while Slim was asleep and still made it back in time to take him to the studio. I learned a lot from Sarge and Roe. They taught me a lot about appearance and conversation as security, about how not to get caught up in the hype. They taught me a lot of survival tactics that I didn't know about.They helped me to take it to the next level. I figured that anybody who could keep Dre alive through all the Death Row drama was worth listening to. California was an educational experience for me about security.

Another thing I learned was that California was a very expensive place to live, and Paul took his time sending out per diems, which are daily allowances. He gave us about $175 a week, which boiled down to about $25 a day, but in California you need double that amount, or at least 35 bucks a day. I told Paul that it was ridiculous that I had to spend my own money for per diems, and every time I spent my own money, I would collect my receipts and send them in for reimbursement.This got to be a hassle because sometimes it took three or four days just to get a response. I told Paul and his accountants to send the per diems out weekly, because they knew how much they were, so they should just send them out. But they didn't. Slim never had any money on him, so I had to dig into my pockets for his liquor, his mistresses' liquor, his tanning booth trips so he could get darker, his food, his haircuts, etc. Now, I'm not a platinum-selling rap artist, so I can't afford the spending habits of one, and I told Paul this. I told Paul, "This boy spends at least $300 a day, and I know y'all reimburse me, but it's hurting me. Y'all need to send me a flat amount of petty cash for this boy so that he has money. Or give me a credit card to hold for him or something."

Paul quickly shot that idea down, saying that I would need power of attorney for that and he didn't want to go through that, and I was like, "But it's OK for me to spend my money on him! I need my money for myself to live! Plus, Slim always loses his cell phone so he stays on mine with his women and his wife, and they call me at all hours of the morning, never saying good morning, just, "Let me speak to Slim!" I would be trying to sleep, so I just started turning my ringer off and giving him the messages as they called. Soon Slim would just ask me where my phone was, and basically my phone became his phone.They would reimburse me, but only after a big hassle over who made what calls. Eventually, they set down a budget for Slim, but it was only $250 a week, and Slim went through that in a day. I was so frustrated because I was Slim's personal bodyguard, not his road manager, not his secretary, not his driver. For the $185 a day that I was making, it wasn't worth it. I brought this up to Paul, telling him that I couldn't keep up with Slim's spending habits, even though they did reimburse me. I told him that I would definitely need a raise for all the various tasks I was performing. I needed more per diem and a raise because I was doing more than my job. I was getting pimped. Again, that idea was shot down. I was like, OK, I settled for the $100 a week, so why am I still here?

I reminded myself of my reason for remaining: for the networking to get my own label off the ground. I was trying to help my own group. No one was doing anything to help me, either. I wasn't even being paid properly for the services that I rendered as a security guard. I was being oppressed, and Paul was the oppressor, and Slim was allowing him to do so. I was allowing myself to be used, because in turn I was using them for something that I didn't have before: the musical connections and the networking. But they were benefiting more from the relationship than I was. They gained a personal security guy, a driver, a chauffeur, and a ho keeper because I kept up with his girls from both coasts. If his wife found out, she would have killed him, just like she will when she reads this book, but who cares? The thing was, he lost his phone and his money, and I kept those things for him because he was as irresponsible as a little kid. He couldn't keep up with anything, and he would lose his head if it wasn't attached. Keeping up with his personal and professional life required me to be paid more than the $185 a day that I was making. It just wasn't worth it doing two or three different peoples' jobs, and I realized that getting certified and better educated about security was the smartest thing I did while I was out in California, doing something that bettered myself.

September 9, 1999, MTV Music Awards

This was a day where again it was shown to me where I stood financially. Paul took the liberty of hiring a guy named Noel, whom he had known for awhile, and he planned to slide this guy into my place as Slim's full-time bodyguard, paying him a rate of $250 a day. I didn't find out about this until later on.When I first met the guy, I didn't care for him too much for the simple reason that Paul had something to do with it. The good thing that came out of this was that Noel had a partner named Rock, whom I had met before and who used to work for Mariah Carey and was currently working for Funkmaster Flex. Rock and I talked, and we exchanged some information, and it turned out that Noel was an OK guy. He was a fair individual. Paul's plans to disrespect me and Noel by trying to slide Noel into my spot backfired because the $250 that I hoped to earn was too small an amount for Noel, and I can understand that because everyone had their own personal rates. Anyway, the three of us became kind of cool by working together, and I always requested them to work with me whenever I worked in New York because I trusted these guys and they were qualified.We would keep in touch over the phone and touch base, as well as keep one another posted on what each of us was making. It turned out that the night of the MTV Music Awards, Rock made $400 and Noel got $250. Now, mind you, I was working 24 hours, and I wasn't making half of what Rock made and didn't even make what Noel made. I didn't blame them in the least because I knew Paul was the one who set everything up. I should have been making what they were making because I had to walk Dre and Slim down the red carpet and deal with all the paparazzi and walk Slim to the bathroom, and even though I got to be on TV, that wasn't my first time being on television, and I'm sure it won't be my last.

Overall, the awards went smoothly until night fell. It was the after-party, and it was hectic because everyone wanted to be in the VIP area. I was thankful for having Rock and Noel there because they really had my back, and I appreciated that. Again, I had nothing against them, but in the back of my mind it pissed me off that Paul was paying them more than me and they were only there for a short period of time. Again, I liked the way Noel and Rock worked, and I always requested to work with them and even requested for them to take my place when I went home on September 11th for my son's birthday.

Prior to my meeting Noel, I met and got cool with one of the head security guys from the Warped Tour named Kenny. He and I kicked it and networked and politicked, and I was going to try to pull him on in my place when I needed days off. The first time I wanted to put him to use was going to be for my son's birthday on the 11th of September, and Paul agreed to that. However, at the last minute Paul decided that it was too expensive to fly Kenny from San Diego to Tampa, and he would rather use Noel. I didn't have a problem with that because I knew Noel would do a good job, but I had a problem with Paul changing his mind at the last minute because Kenny had turned down other work to take this job. That put a damper on my friendship with Kenny. I mean, we still kick it, and he understands that I had nothing to do with it, but it comes to mind every time we talk. It was just another example of Paul being unprofessional. He doesn't care how his actions affect other people or whether they are to anyone else's liking. It didn't bother me that Noel did the job. It bothered me that Paul couldn't tell Kenny the truth the first time when he gave Kenny the job, because Kenny missed out on a $1,500 job elsewhere. Paul took advantage of every opportunity he could to step on the toes of as many people as he could, especially security guys, as you'll find out.

After my son's birthday, I returned to California in mid-September, while Slim continued working on his second album. It was business as usual, with me taking him here and there, spending my money, calling his hos, making his appointments—it was to the point where it almost seemed normal. I called Paul to get the remaining itinerary for September. I wanted to make some personal plans. My wife's birthday was coming up, and I didn't want to miss it. I had already missed our wedding anniversary in May, as well as my son's christening, and I was beginning to realize that some moments were lost forever. I was making a strong effort to at least not miss any birthdays. I had just purchased my home that year and had not been able to spend three weeks in it at one time. I was getting sick of sleeping in the hotels, eating the hotel food, and living out of a suitcase. Again I wasn't feeling

Em pops the top during a fourteen hour delay in DC on the way to Europe.

respected or appreciated, and I knew I was constantly improving myself yet wasn't being recognized for it. I didn't care if they liked me or not, but they would have to respect me. I always had a doubt in my mind that they didn't respect me.We had Hawaii coming up, with the Dre–Snoop "Break Up to Make Up" reunion there, so I made arrangements to have my wife come out that Thursday, the 23rd, so she could go to Hawaii, as well.

Then something really pissed me off. All I asked them to do was to have a car waiting for her. I had the key to the room for her at the front desk, but I knew I would be too busy running around to pick her up. She didn't know anyone in California. I talked to Dean Geislinger, who handled all the accounts as far as the limos, and he supposedly made arrangements for her to be picked up. He is a pretty decent guy. I don't know if there was a mistake on his part or some other outside factors, but, needless to say, there was no car waiting for my wife the night she arrived. She ended up having to take a taxi, and she was afraid because neither one of us knew the area too well. I wasn't asking for a limo or anything extravagant, just a simple car to transport her safely. They couldn't even do that much. It was just a big mess. You would think that for all I did for them they could get one thing right.

As you will read later, Hawaii turned out to be trouble in paradise. My wife stayed an extra day but left after all the drama that you will read about shortly. Anyway, when we returned home from Hawaii, we started getting calls that we may have had to go back to Europe.We did a 10-day promo tour there in August, and we weren't looking forward to going back. The tour was light work, and it was cool to see Europe for the first time, but it wasn't exactly the type of place where you wanted to spend weeks at a time. Slim couldn't stand it—he hated Europe. I learned to hate it, too, at least from the aspect of visiting it on business with Slim Shady.

It was October 7th, about a week before we were scheduled to leave for Europe, and I was under stress and underpaid. I was reaching a boiling point from dealing with all the various forms of stress that came with the territory of working with Slim. I felt that I had proven myself to the Shady Tours family many times, and in many ways, and that I was worth more than I was being paid, and I was still not receiving the respect that I felt due. This was the first time I ever chewed Paul's ass out. I had tried by all available forms of communication to reach Paul: phone, cell phone, pager, and e-mail—you name it. He was unresponsive to all my efforts. Slim was getting impatient with me because I had no money—which meant he had no money—and Paul was not reimbursing me or getting back to me in response to all the messages I had left him.

I took the liberty of writing Paul a two-page letter telling him about everything from the lack of money to the lack of respect that I was dealing with. I told him how I felt about being on the road six or seven weeks at a time and only being able to hear my wife's and kids' voices. I was seldom allowed any time off. He didn't care about the drama I was going through in California, dealing with Death Row and Slim's personal life. He didn't care about the stumbling blocks I was going through or the strain my absence was putting on my marriage. I was on the road raising Slim, a grown man, when I needed some time to be at home and raise my own kids. I was too busy trying to cultivate this man and help him keep himself together. I felt a lot of guilt for giving this man all of my attention and not being appreciated when I belonged at home, where I would be appreciated, even though I would only be able to stay for a short time.That really affected my kids and my wife. My wife told me that my older son couldn't even sleep at night, and he would just wake up and cry for no reason. My biggest fear was that I would come home from a six-month stint and my baby boy wouldn't even know me.

I had sacrificed a lot and gained little.You can't go back in time and regain the moments you missed. I began to analyze what was important. I looked to my Bible for the answers because no one around me could really sense what I was going through. I had always been into my Bible, but I was really leaning on it now. Dealing with Paul and Slim, you had to pray, because if you didn't you would wind up killing one of them boys. That's the main reason I kept reading the Bible, that and for my own salvation. I'll admit I made some mistakes on the road and got caught in the hype. All security guards at one time or another get caught in the hype, if they're not careful. I realized how easy it was to cross the line. It doesn't take more than a minute. But some security guards get caught up and never catch themselves. If you catch yourself and recuperate from it, you're OK. I made some mistakes, and one of those mistakes was drinking. I admit it, I am human.

My first big mistake was being in Amsterdam. Amsterdam was full of drugs. I experimented with some hash brownies and drank some mushroom tea and also went to a live sex show. I got a little out of character, and it was because I needed an escape from the problems I was going through and to escape the guilt I felt from being away from my wife and kids. When I left Amsterdam, I felt like shit. While I was there, I was still into my Bible, but I was in this mode like,Yo, I'm going to have me some fun! That attitude cost me some of my dignity and definitely cost me some of my pride. No one in the crew held it against me.They were all getting high because that was what Amsterdam was all about: all the drugs you could take and all the sex you could want. The hash brownies tasted just like brownie,s only they had weed in them; the mushroom tea tasted just like regular tea only it was shrooms instead. I even smoked a little weed. I was out of character, but I admit it. It's sad to say that is one of the only times when Slim and Paul showed me any respect, because I was on their level then, I was on a lower level. Being caught up in the hype is not a good thing because it gets you out of character. I am not the only one who got out of character. I saw Paul, a lawyer, taking Ecstasy and doing Whip-Its, which are little balloons of nitrous oxide that are sucked up through a metal canister, and they freeze your brain and kill your brain cells. I saw Paul smoke weed. I heard some people say that they were going to call the bar association because they had seen Paul out in public places taking drugs. I didn't judge him because that was what he chose to do. Personally, I felt as if I had diminished my pride and my dignity to an extent, because I felt as though I had sidetracked myself from what I was trying to accomplish, that I had stooped to their level, and that the one time I stooped to their level, they actually respected me. It was odd, because it indicated that they believed that I thought I was better than them because I never had a drink. If I did have a drink, it was in my room at night while Slim was asleep. I never got drunk because I had a job to do, and Slim was always unpredictable. If he got up in the middle of the night and wanted to go to a club or something, how would I look sitting up there drunk? I only had a drink at times when I wanted to unwind.

After the first time in Amsterdam, I realized that no one is perfect, especially me, but I knew that I wouldn't make the same mistake twice. So, I really got into myself and stayed in my Bible. I wasn't trying to be perfect, I was only trying to maintain.With so much stuff going on, my stress level was way too high, and I was just trying to deal. The thrill of touring was gone. I had been on three tours with Slim. I did the Slim Shady Tour in April, the Warped Tour for five weeks in the summer, and the 10-day European promo tour. Between tours, we were traveling between recording studios. I needed to have a talk with Slim about some things that were building up.We never had an off-the-record one-on-one talk between us before. At this time, we were approaching the time to go home. It was October 14th, and his birthday was coming up on the 17th. I figured I had nothing to lose by having a talk with him because I had heard he was having some personal problems of his own. He was feeling that his wife was cheating on him because she would never let him stay with her when he went home, and she was never home when he called her from the road. She used Hailey as a tool against him. He couldn't even drive his own truck whenever he was at home because his wife always had it.

Big-Naz, Eminem and Proof: Love, peace, and shrooms!

The only common ground they had was their daughter, and any other time they dealt with each other, they were literally fighting. He married her at the end of June during the first tour, for what reason I do not know, because if you don't get along in the first place then you only make the problem worse if you get married. The tour had taken its toll on him because he realized that Paul was keeping him so busy—in order to keep his own pockets fat—that he didn't have time to see his own daughter. This is how I opened up the conversation with him. I said, "Look man, I know we have this second European tour coming up, but I am burnt out, man. I can't do it." He didn't take that too well at all, but I didn't care. I said, "This is off the record, but my marriage is suffering, and my kids need me. We are both good fathers and everything, but we don't even have time to see our children. I can't do it." I said, "My son just asked me who was going to protect him while I was protecting Slim Shady, and my answer to that was God. He didn't want to hear that though, because all he knew was that he wanted his daddy home. I tried to explain to him what my job was, but he was convinced that I worked at the airport because that was always the last place where he saw me when they dropped me off."

My family's needs were returning to being top priority over my personal goals—it was just going to take longer than I wanted for my group and label to get off the ground. But I realized that I already had everything that I had ever dreamed of in my family. Some people think that money is the key to happiness, but you can have all the money in the world and still be miserable. Look at Slim—he has money, and he is the most miserable man I know. I told him that I needed to get my house back in order.That I needed to be with my family and that they needed me there. Slim probably didn't understand that because he was newly married, and I knew that as soon as Slim married Kim that it was going to be a mess because she was a bitch.I mean,look in the dictionary under "bitch" and you'll see a picture of Kimberly Scott.Anyway, I weighed the pros and the cons of my being on the road and doubted that it was even worth the trouble for me being miserable, underpaid, and away from my family. I was looking at and I said, "Right now, let me be honest with you. Right now, you have no life. I know you want to be a better father than your father was to you, because you didn't even know your father. Straight up, you are already that because you acknowledge your daughter and you are out here working so that she doesn't have to work a day in her life. But Kim is your downfall. She is holding you back, and for some reason you can't let her go. But right now, in my eyes, I have more than you do. I have a wife who supports me, I just bought a house, I have two nice cars, a nice job, and I had all of this stuff before I met you.You, Slim, you just sold two million plus records, and you are living like you are still washing dishes at Gilbert's. Man, you got to stop that shit; you have an image to uphold. I'm not saying that you got to have everything iced out, but damn! You got that truck that she is driving, so you might as well give it to her, plus it's got that bigass dent in it that you haven't had fixed yet.

"When you go home, you are staying over at her mom's house, sleeping in a fucking twin bunk bed with Kim on the bottom and you on the top. Man, you are living like you are poor! She wants you to get her this apartment? Man, fuck that! What about Slim? No, fuck that, too! What about what Marshall wants? You need to get you something and stop living like you are poor, man. Stop living like you are a fucking bum!" That is one of the few times that he and I were on the same page—both frustrated and both needing to get our homes and relationships in order. I think I was the first person who talked to Slim about those things on that level, and he really got on Paul's back. Slim said, "I don't give a fuck about the money! Cancel this European tour!" He really tried to have it canceled, but with Paul being greedy, he wouldn't do it because it would affect his 20 percent. That was the first time I saw those two at odds. Slim got on Paul about keeping him so busy he didn't have time to do shit. But Paul, not having any kids, didn't understand the concept or realize the importance of family. He's greedy. He's all about the money. That's just the type of person he is.

3

CALIFORNIA STRESS

I quickly found out that all of my dreams of trying to get my own label off the ground could be put on hold forever because I was put in a dangerous situation. The first time I realized how deep things were in this security thing dealing with Death Row was at the 1999 Source Awards in mid-August out in Los Angeles. Going there, I hadn't any gripes about anything. Rather, I was naive about the situation because I figured that Slim didn't have anything to do with what had been going on between Death Row and Dre in the past. I was more concerned with Slim mouthing off to somebody he had dissed on a record or something. I was expecting something more along those lines because I knew a lot of people didn't care for him too much, but they had to give him his props because the boy is tight lyrically, no doubt. You can't take nothing from him on that, but a lot of people didn't like him because he's a white boy out here rhyming and doing his thing, but you got to give credit when it's due. That day at the Source Awards, I remember it being hot out, with all the stars coming out like Don King, Mike Tyson, Janet Jackson, Hot Boys — everybody; you name them, they were there, from the NBA players to the movie stars.

It was cool to see a lot of black folks coming out supporting one another. But, I must say, the Source Awards are too damn "ghetto" for

Studio session for the Marshall Mathers LP with Dre and Xzibit in West Hollywood.

me, and too "ghetto" to be televised. Luckily, they were able to go back and edit certain parts before they actually showed it "live," as it was prerecorded, because some of the things that went down were ridiculous. But before I get into that...we pulled up in the limo and had to do the red carpet walk and everything. It was pretty cool, and all I had to do was make sure I kept close to Slim. Mind you, at this point in time I was just working with Slim as a shield, using my mental capabilities and physical skills like judo or martial arts to protect him, but, for the most part, I was dealing with groupies and pulling him out of the crowd. I was basically deterring situations, even though the physical defense mechanisms were there ready to be used at any given time, even though we tried to talk our way out of any given situation. I wasn't really expecting any problems, with the exception of one or two people who I knew didn't like him because of some things he said on his record about their personal problems, but that's part of the business and comes with the game. A lot of people were showing him some love and giving him pounds when he was walking through and shaking hands and whatnot. A lot of people were conversing with him. "I want to do a song with you," said a

The after-effects of the drama preceding the Source Awards. Aug. 1999.

few emcees. I thought it was cool because I didn't expect him to get that much love from so many people. I could tell was it real. They were congratulating him on his success. Once we got inside, we learned the seating arrangements were all mixed up. They only had three seats available for Slim, when other acts had at least five to ten. One seat went to Eminem, one went to Proof, his hype man, and the third one went to his A&R person. I should have been sitting there because at a predominantly black event, nine times out of ten there's going to be some drama. There's always one fool in every bunch, especially with a lot of young black folks who are making money who like mouthing off. Lo and behold, that fool showed himself that night. I couldn't sit with Slim due to the seating arrangement. None of the security guards were able to sit with their principal, the person they were guarding. Dre's security guard was having the same problem. That night I wasn't dressed as a security person because when I go places I like to dress as comfortably as possible, in this case as comfortably as Slim. I noticed the attire Sarge and Rowe had on—these guys came in all-black military fatigues looking like they were straight from the SWAT team—they were very impressive, and

Byron posing with Hollywood Porn celebs who gave the crew a freak show.

they had an intimidating presence.They weren't as big as me, but the way they were dressed, their composure, the whole nine impressed me and I learned a lot from them. They basically taught me that I needed to dress the part, so that people will know that I am security and will think twice before approaching me—because of the vibe given off—before any problems could occur. I don't think my attire, though, had anything to do with what might have gone down that night, and it definitely wouldn't have prepared me for what happened next.

As I was standing off to the side, the show was going on, and they were doing the taping and stuff, and I saw how "ghetto" the experience really was. For example, they had Dre present an award, but when they gave him the paper to present the award, there was nothing on it. Thank God it wasn't live because there was literally a five-minute delay between the time it took them to find out who the winner was and Dre to announce it. Luckily, they were able to edit that part out. By the time Dre was on, there were several Death Row guys, all dressed in red T-shirts, sitting in the same section that Slim was in about eight rows back. Of course, they noticed him walk in, but I don't think they noticed he had security because, again, I wasn't able to sit with him and had to sit on the opposite side against a wall and watch him, as well as the people around him, and see what his reaction was. About an hour into the show, during a commercial break, Slim got up and signaled to me that he was going to the restroom. I had him wait while I walked around the long way, since I couldn't go straight to him because the rows were filled. I had to walk up the opposite aisle, go into the hallway, come back into the facility, and meet him halfway in the aisle. I was trying to wade through all these people and, mind you, it was the Source Awards—it was very crowded, everybody was trying to show up in their outfits, their platinum chains, their Rolexes, the whole nine. I could see Slim getting congratulations from some more people, but before I could reach him, there were several guys in red T-shirts who approached him. I wasn't thinking that this could be a Death Row-related issue, due to the laid-back atmosphere; it was just a lot of black folks mingling.

I was still making my way through the crowd trying to get to Slim. The whole time, I was watching his face. These guys in red T-shirts were talking to him, and Slim was talking back to them, and I suddenly saw Slim's facial expression change from a mild mannered to an angry—Slim turned flush red; he was just as red as the Death Row guys'T-shirts. I was about three feet from him. I could hear the argument between Slim and the lead guy from Death Row. From what I understood, this guy ranked high. I was working my way through the last of the crowd when I heard the lead guy say, "What's that Death Row like?" And Slim said, "What are you talking about, what's that Death Row like?" They went on repeating, "Death Row, muh fucka, Death Row!" "How you like that Death Row?! We up in here, muh fucka!" By the time I reached Slim, he was agitated to the point where he was ready to swing. The Death Row guys were all up in Slim's face. I pushed the lead guy back and put Slim behind. I asked, "What's the deal, man? What's going on? We can't be having any of this shit up in here!" A Death Row guy responded, "Who the fuck is you?!!" "I'm Slim's security, and we aren't going to be having no problems up in here!" Now at this time, it hadn't really registered yet that these cats were from Death Row. Next thing I knew, they were hollering, "Death Row, muh fucka! You gon' see us again." Immediately, I got Slim out of there. We went into the hallway, and by that time he was amped.

Slim's fists were balled up, and he was nervous and scared. Honestly, I was nervous because they had outnumbered us, plus we were on their turf. I held my ground though. In the midst of getting him out of there, it dawned on me this was Death Row we were dealing with here. I expected some drama here—but not with Death Row Records. They are the last ones you want to get into it with. I said, "Alright, we got to deal with this situation!" The first thing I did was get on the phone and notify Paul of what had just happened. I informed Dean (Slim's A&R rep) to go tell Dre's security what was going on, as well.We knew we had to act fast. We had to get in and present the award for DMX, so we couldn't leave.We were escorted downstairs to the holding area for the people to present the awards. The whole time I was looking out for anyone from Death Row. So many people were still coming up to Slim giving him play. I was thinking, somebody is going to try to steal on him. I was Slim's only security guy. Prior to the Source Awards, I kept telling Paul that we were going to need additional security. I also suggested bulletproof vests be purchased for Slim and myself. I stressed that to him so many times weeks before the Source Awards happened. I was looking to be on the safe side, because Slim has talked so much shit about so many people in his songs. If history serves me correctly, someone has always gotten shot or killed after the Source Awards or after the Soul Train Awards.

I didn't want take that chance of Slim being the next target. He was vulnerable due to his high visibility—a white kid doing black music and talking shit about a lot of people. I was putting two and two together, taking preventive measures. Paul always shot down security measures, which wasn't his job, although Slim gave him the okay to make the final call. His response was, "Naz, we are not trying to portray that type of image with Slim wearing a bulletproof vest. It wouldn't be

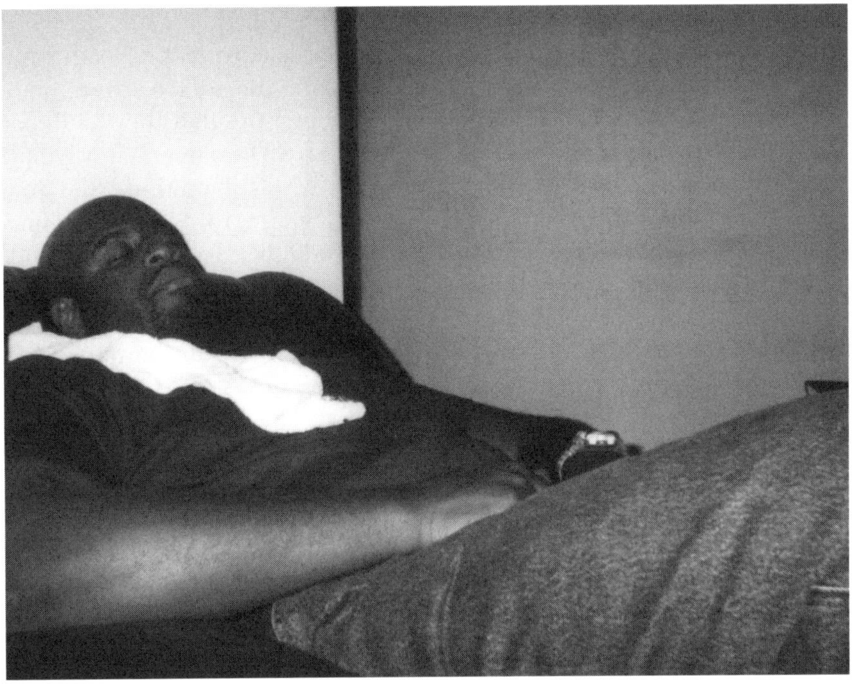

Byron takes a quick nap after the Source Awards drama.

cordial or appropriate for him to go into the Source Awards with a bulletproof vest on." My response was, "Paul, look at the past Source Awards, the problems, the beefs, the skirmishes. Look at the Soul Train Awards, the after-parties, all these hiphop artists there. It always ends with somebody getting shot or killed. Look at the last few years!" He still said he didn't think it was wise to do that. So now, with all the drama jumpin' off, Paul was alerted that Death Row Records had approached us and tried to intimidate us. Paul was scared shitless! Slim was fuckin' trippin' at that point. Slim couldn't figure out why they were harassing him. I was looking at the situation like, damn! I go from reading about this Death Row shit to being in the middle of it. What the fuck am I doing here? It was like a "Twilight Zone" moment; I could hear the "Twilight Zone" music playing. I said to myself, What the hell just happened? What just happened?

We realized that we had bitten off more than we could chew. We didn't expect this magnitude of drama—and it only got worse. Eventually, Slim presented DMX the award. Immediately afterward, I notified the limo driver by radio about what had gone on and asked him to pull up. Meanwhile, I was trying to get Slim together. I was bringing him out of a back room so we could avoid contact with the Death Row guys again.We got word that they were looking for us. They were definitely looking to start some shit. Later, we found out that they had beef with Slim because of Slim's affiliation with Dre. Dr. Dre previously had a beef with Death Row.To them, Slim was the next best thing, the new kid on the block, the most vulnerable. At this point, I was really trippin' because I didn't have any backup. Dre and his security did their thing, and they bounced. I couldn't blame them because they really hadn't had any face-to-face dealings that night. I focused on staying calm and not being nervous. If they see you nervous, they will really bother you. I finally got Slim out of there. I saw the limo pull up—then pull off—leaving me, Paul, and Slim standing in the front. The driver had been told to move, that he couldn't sit there. He had only been sitting there like thirty seconds!

The red carpet security didn't listen to the driver's explanation of what had happened. Then words were being exchanged between the outside security and myself.They didn't care that a man's life could be in danger. Due to the traffic, it took the limo driver ten minutes to go around the block and come back to us. During this ten minutes, Paul was turning red because he was so scared, and Slim was freaking out trying to figure out why they would want a piece of him. I was trying to watch my back and Slim's. I tried to keep him calm. Slim kept saying, "We're fucked, man! We're fucked!" Paul humbly said, "Naz, I think you were right, we should have gotten those vests." I said, "Paul, we discussed this weeks ago. I told you we needed vests and that I would need some additional help! You shut down every idea that I presented to you. Please don't even bring up the woulda-coulda-shoulda. I already made this clear to you." Paul and Slim didn't understand the importance of security. I think that was the first time they really realized it. Finally, the car came back.

Slim was mad as hell. He was pacing, drawing attention to himself, saying, "Man, these guys are gonna come up and shoot us right here on the spot!" I mean, he was really freakin' out, and I was trying to calm him down. "If a paparazzi sees this and doesn't know what is going on, they could make it a bigger issue than it is. It's big right now, but don't get the media involved. When the limo finally arrives, let's just get in the limo, then wave at your fans, and let's bounce, man. Let's get the fuck out of here! When the limo pulls up, we'll all jump in." Proof got in the limo and said, "Yo, Naz man, you was right about those vests, man." Now everyone agreed with me—afterward—that we should have gotten those bulletproof vests for the 1999 Source Awards out in LA. It felt so good to get in that limo and pull out alive. When you're on someone else's turf, you don't really know what's going down, you don't really know how folks are laying. I was just out there doing a job. I had no knowledge of what we were dealing with.

That was the first confrontation we had with Death Row Records. I must say, that was a unforgettable moment. I didn't know what was going to happen next.The only thing that kept playing through my mind was the shooting of Biggie Smalls in California, then the shooting of Tupac Shakur in Vegas. You never know how things are going to turn out. I have to say that made me real nervous, but it me made smarter.

I quickly learned about LA, California, and the dress code.You hear about things on the news, you hear a lot of hearsay, you hear a lot of stuff on people's records, and, from what I understand, the red means Bloods and the blue means Crips. Being from Detroit, none of that shit really registers with me. I don't follow none of that, but when you are in their territory you have to respect it; it's real and you got to respect it. I changed my wardrobe during my two-month stay in LA—there was no red, and there was no blue. I always found myself wearing a lot of gray, a lot of black, and a lot of beige. It's a damn shame it has to be like that but that's how it is when you go out to Cali! You have to pack accordingly, especially in the field of work that I'm in. I'm around a lot of those gangstas all the time. Whatever their affiliation was, I respected that. Being from Detroit, we don't get off into gang banging.

After the Source Awards, we went to the studio; Slim wanted to do some recording. He tried to do some recording, but he couldn't really focus. Slim was shaken up from the Death Row situation. First thing I did when we got back to the studio usually was read a book. I had some downtime when we were at the studio, and I usually read during that period. I felt very ignorant about what was going on, and nobody in the business out there really wanted to talk about the history of Death Row, plus the history of the gang life. I took the initiative to find out, because you can't really be out there and not know what's going on. I was basically already sitting in California naked, meaning with no guns and no vest. I was basically out there with my wits and the Lord's Prayer. That's what kept me alive—the Lord! I was reading my Bible and working my wits.

I have plenty of street smarts.You can't go out there and disrespect their culture, because if you do you are definitely going to have some problems. I had a sleepless night, spent trying to figure out what was going on and what was going to happen, and grasping the fact that I was in the middle of some bullshit that I didn't really know anything about. Regardless, I was in the middle of it and had to deal with it. The next morning, I got up bright and early, went and had some breakfast, and found a bookstore and bought this book called *Have Gun Will Travel* by Ronin Ro. Basically, this book was built on interviews from Death Row members, members of Interscope, and people from Loud Records and tells of their encounters with Death Row. It tells about the rise and fall of Death Row Records, about Bad Boy, and also about the killing of Tupac Shakur and Biggie Smalls. It tells about the good times and the bad times. Basically, it covers about ten years of hip-hop, and tells how Death Row was formed, how Suge used to help out artists who were getting screwed over, and how he went in and straightened everything out. It mentioned a lot of good things and a lot of bad things, and it answered every question I had and made things a lot clearer to me. What I realized was, OK, this is why Interscope acts like this with this group of guys, and this is why this guy is in the studio doing this and so on and so forth. I felt like I wasn't completely in the dark anymore, but I knew I had a lot to learn. It took me about a week to read this book, and I read a lot of chapters over and over to get a feel for how these Death Row guys think. Being from Detroit, there's a different way of thinking.You have to respect their mentality out there. You might not like it or agree with it, but you are going to respect it.You must abide if you are going to survive.

I did some research on California gangsters. I studied their approach. I don't know if this is factual, but from what I've read and what I've seen, they always approach a person with some conversation first, to see where your head is at and to see where your heart is. And the next time they are on some intimidation shit, and if you aren't feeling what they are saying, then God help you. And I can honestly say staying in my Bible and staying focused helped me through it. No disrespect to Death Row, I am just explaining the situation that I went through with them. If I got beef with anybody, it's with Paul and Slim for paying me $185 a day to be dealing with that shit, plus doing extra work that I wasn't supposed to be doing. Now you tell me if $185 is worth all that—hell no—not in anybody's life. Being certified and qualified at that time, I said,Yo, it's time for me to act a little bit quicker to get some more things under my belt, making things happen. So, at this point in time, we were a little shook up, and we were nervous because we had to stay out in LA. I brought the situation to the table to Jimmy Iovine and told him what was going on, but he blew the whole thing off like, "Oh, those guys, they're always doing that.They're just fucking with you guys, they're just trying to intimidate you. Don't worry about it. I'll talk to them. I'll tell Suge to tell those guys to stop fucking with you because Suge is not sending those guys to do that." I said, "Even if he's not, the point is they are from Death Row Records, and they are fucking with us. I mean damn, man, how are we supposed to take that? We're just out here so Slim can finish his album." I was just trying to get this man back to his daughter and his wife safely, that was my whole task.

I just kept getting frustrated because everybody kept blowing it off like, "Aw, man, don't worry about it. It isn't no big deal, they do this shit all the time." I'm like, "Yo, I'm not about to take no chances like that, man! I can't afford to take no chances without knowing what's going on." So shortly after that we went home for about a week or so to kind of let things cool off out there, and Slim did some recording here at home. I was home and really looking at this situation and I'm like, Yo, man, this situation is really getting crazy man, this shit is getting crazy! I don't want to be involved in something this crazy. I'm just trying to make some money; I'm just trying to get my label on. I was trying to get the Wadsquad out by doing something independent myself. I didn't realize how hard it was going to be to get that done.

More Stress

During our stay in California, I decided to go to school. I figured with all the drama building, I better be prepared for the worst. Every morning, from 8:00 a.m. to 1:00 p.m., I attended a law enforcement academy that certified me in executive protection. This process took two months to complete.This was done on my own out of loyalty to Slim.This certification would allow me to carry a concealed weapon legally throughout the US. I was certified to kill, but only if my life or my client's life were in endangered. I was granted arrest powers, as well. In doing this, I felt that my stock should go up and requested a raise. Paul took the liberty to thank me for my efforts in protecting Slim and then denied the raise.They even denied reimbursement for my certification. I just continued to roll with the punches. My job went beyond being his bodyguard. I was his part-time assistant, part-time accountant, chauffeur, mentor, main supporter, and friend. I went beyond the call of duty. I was the only one that had some control over his negative impulses. However, as he blew up, so did his head. Paul did his best to keep up the confusion between Slim and I. I was partially used as Paul's fall guy until I wised up. There were times in California where I would spend my own money on Slim, because Paul and Slim's accountant didn't want him to have money. And when Slim did have money, he would lose it all. He'd lose his head if it wasn't attached. Over a period of time, Slim lost about $1,200, three cell phones, and a few verses to songs—and it usually fell back on me to do the searching. Overall, Slim was a decent guy at times.

He would try to sign every autograph until everyone was satisfied. There were times when he seemed human. For example, he wanted to watch Ice-T perform from the crowd, even though he was on the same tour. I made it happen. He was like little kid at a concert for the first time. Nobody bothered him. There were difficult times, like when I refused to take part in his drug activities. I never liked him using the drugs, because I didn't want the responsibility of notifying the next of kin if he OD'd. A few years ago, I was a drug treatment counselor and, from my analysis, Slim had all the symptoms of an abuser. It's no secret. I can recall one day during the Warp Tour where he took fourteen different drugs. It started with Ecstasy, then liquor, Vicodin, Valium, shrooms, marijuana,Tylenol 3, Whip-Its, and a host of other overthe- counter drugs. He was scared to go to sleep that night. Then there were times when he would be selective and claim he was cutting back. "Today I'm only doing Ecstasy!" Slim would say.That would last for twelve hours. I've always seen Slim as an unloved little boy who throws tantrums. He has to have his way or everyone will be miserable. One time we were running late for a flight, and he had to have a vegetarian Whopper from Burger King.We missed the flight! Needless to say, Paul wasn't happy.

Slim can be very bold at times, like when were in San Diego. There was this mother and two teenage kids who claimed they were his stepfamily from his dad. They made it known that they didn't want anything from him, they just wanted to be acknowledged. This family had pictures of Slim's dad and themselves. The photos had a very strong resemblance to Marshall. I was given the honor to present this to Slim to see if he was interested in meeting them. He glanced at the photos and said he didn't want anything to do with his dad. He then turned and threw the photos out the bus window where the family was waiting. The crew tried to convince him to at least hear their story, but he refused. It was sad because that might have been his only chance to learn about his dad. But in retrospect his father might have set the whole thing up. Who knows?

4

TROUBLE IN PARADISE

Death Row at the Dr. Dre Break Up to Make Up Reunion, September 24, 1999. My wife and I were out, as kind of a make-up thing for me having to miss her birthday due to touring. My wife, the whole Shady Tours crew, and I were loaded up to go to Hawaii, a six-hour flight from LA. It was a beautiful flight going out, and everybody was having fun talking about what they were going to do: this, that, and the other. That changed very quickly because as soon as the plane doors opened, airport security and Honolulu police were there to escort us from our airplane safely to our vehicles, telling us they would send our luggage later. We couldn't figure out what was going on, we just thought they were giving us extra escorts. But they were like, "No, we are coming to inform you that there are like thirty guys here from Death Row Records, and from what we understand they were on the same plane as Snoop Dogg, and they were antagonizing him, talking some shit." I'm thinking, Man, we are in Hawaii, trying to chill! Damn! The whole mood went from having a good time to drama. When the plane doors opened, everything changed. It was like we walked into a jungle of fire. Things just got hot quickly, and I'm telling myself, This shit is not happening! This is not happening. Immediately, I'm thinking, OK I need to send my wife back home. She is going to be mad, but this shit is about to get ugly. Anytime you got thirty Death Row guys flying from Cali to Hawaii to try to start some shit, to try to pause the Break Up to Make Up Reunion, man you know there's about to be some shit. That took some masterful planning. Anybody that does that, you got to have much respect for. You got to have much respect for that because that's organized. They got long arms!! That told me right there that they could reach out anywhere at any given time and get to you, whether it be Dre, Snoop, or Eminem. They didn't give a fuck! I learned that real quickly. SHIT! I was totally blown away. And if I had to say there was one time I was scared, that was the time, because they caught me totally by surprise for the second time. I wasn't expecting to see them there. You know, you are in Hawaii and you are expecting to enjoy the beach, the sun, the food, but all that shit quickly changed.The whole setting changed because everyone went from, "Ahh, Hawaii" to "Oh, shit!" It was ugly. Finally, we got Honolulu police and airport security to escort us to our vehicle. Immediately Sarge and Rowe put Dre in a van at the back of the airport where Death Row couldn't see them, and they fled. They busted up.They are pretty good at handling stuff like that. Me, I was only one person and didn't have a second person I could set up and organize with or anything. It was just me, and I had to do everything at the same time as watching Slim. It was pretty hectic. Unfortunately, we had to go out the front door. There were some police officers that were working with us as extra added security coming from California. So we had to wait a while because some had to get their guns and their vests, which were still in their luggage. They lost my luggage, but I didn't have anything in it anyway, but the whole point was we are here in Hawaii, Death Row is out here, and they are starting shit. It was instant stress and instant drama. I was freaking out because I was mad now. I had invited my wife to come out, and I knew she was going to have an attitude, so I was worried about her, and I had to worry about Slim, who was crazy. The happy mood was broken. Everybody got their luggage except me; they sent mine later to the hotel.We all got in the van, and the mood went from everybody talking about having fun and chasing women to complete silence. I mean, all you saw was everybody putting on their bulletproof vests, loading and cocking their Glocks, pulling back their hammers, the whole nine, checking their guns, and all you could hear was "click-click, snap, pop."We were like, damn! About half a block down all you could see were these red-and-black jerseys; these guys had on strictly red and black. It was them Death Row cats.

They had made it known that they were in the house, and it worked. So we pulled off in the van, with the Honolulu police as an escort, and headed to our hotel. The drama began at the hotel. Immediately, we had switched Snoop from the hotel he was at, which was the venue where they were going to be performing a show in the banquet hall. Death Row was apparently staying at the same hotel where Snoop was, so we had to get Snoop from that hotel to our hotel, and we had the Honolulu police surround the perimeter of the whole hotel. Anybody who looked like they didn't belong there was stopped and questioned, people from Xzibit to Snoop to Dre to their wives to their girlfriends to their kids. No one could leave the premises without proper escort. It was basically demanded that no one go anywhere. I think we were on the best part of the island, and we got the best hotel on the beach, so everything we needed was right there on the spot—the bar, the swimming pool, everything. We really didn't have to go anywhere, but it just rained on the whole parade. We were all confined to our rooms, and all the artists, such as Xzibit, Dre, Snoop, and Eminem, had to have two police officers on twelve-hour shifts outside of their rooms. Anytime we went anywhere we had numerous bodyguards, so there were a good twelve bodyguards among us, and there were like, two police officers for every two bodyguards. We were deep, so basically we outnumbered them, but it was just the point of being uncomfortable.

We couldn't go anywhere, we couldn't sleep in peace, and we were worried about the drama, what was going to happen next. I had my wife here trying to celebrate her birthday. It was miserable, but we made the most of it. My thing was in a situation like that you worry about the women because they are the weakest link. I guess my mind really got the best of me because I was thinking, They're going to target me because I'm Slim's bodyguard, and he's the new guy, and the way to him is get to me. I brought my wife along, and it's her birthday, and they might try to approach her. I was just really tripping' out at this point. Now, I knew to expect the unexpected whenever I was with Slim. "Yo, this shit is getting crazy." I couldn't deal with it, you know. Everybody was stressed out. Folks were mad, people were miserable, everybody's women had attitudes, and you couldn't blame them because it was supposed to be a time in paradise, but it turned into a time of terror in Hawaii. We finally got everything situated and organized and secured the premises. Every artist's door was secure on a 24-hour basis. And then some of the drama began. The second night, we had to do a sound check for the show and, mind you, the sound check was at the same hotel where Death Row was staying, and they tried to bombard the facility; they tried to bum-rush the sound check, and there were quite a few of them. The numbers were pretty equal, you could figure, between the artists and the bodyguards; maybe we had them outnumbered by about ten or fifteen guys. But my

MC Proof and Slim clowning around in Paris, France.

point was that these guys weren't from Hawaii but flew from California to start some shit, and they were organized. From what I understood, they had two off-duty police offcers that were down with them to basically help them get through a lot of the bullshit. A couple of the security personnel knew this and notified hotel security not to let these guys on the premises period, even though they stayed in the hotel, and not to let them anywhere near the banquet level.

When everyone from Dre's camp, Xzibit's camp, and Snoop's camp all found out that Death Row was trying to bombard the sound check, they went downstairs to confront the issue, but the police stopped it and sent everybody back up, and I was just like, Yo, I'm staying with Slim because he isn't trying to run off. I was just holding him down and letting him know what was going on, and he was kind of nervous—and drinking to ease his nerves—and from that point on it was just really nerve-racking because we didn't know what to expect. That night during the show, we had to get back on extra watch because these guys made the statement that they were going to rush the stage, and none of the bodyguards that night could have their weapons because of a hotel security rule. And the police officers were the only ones allowed to carry weapons. But it went down pretty smoothly. The only problem I ran into was one of the police escorts disappeared on us, the one who was supposed to take us out to our van through the back way out the venue. It was really upsetting Slim, it really bothered me, and I chewed that guy's ass something terrible because he was supposed to be working under our command. We had hired the Honolulu Police Department specifically to follow what we requested them to do. It wasn't ego tripping, but our lives were at stake, and we didn't have room for any mistakes, and when this guy didn't meet us where he was supposed to meet us, it made me real nervous, and it made Slim nervous. We had to sit and wait on this guy, and I finally decided, hey, we're going to move without this guy. We couldn't take these kinds of chances because we had to beat the mob out of there because there was going to be a crowd of people as far as groupies and whatnot, and if Death Row was going to do something, that would be the opportune time to do it. We left about fifteen minutes before the show actually ended.

We got in our van and had a police escort take us back. Everything went pretty smoothly up to that point, even though the situation was still nerve-racking, without having the original Honolulu police escort there. I had all kinds of thoughts going through my mind, like maybe they paid this guy off, why was this guy missing at this point in time? You know? He had a radio, and I had been talking to him on the radio, so there was no form of miscommunication, so where was he?

But eventually he did show up at the hotel, and you should have seen us, it was incredible the way we were moving! For the first time, I didn't have anybody lagging behind, and my big thing was keeping my wife near me. I told her stay near me; even though I was working with Slim she should stay near me. I had to keep an eye on her, too. It made my job kind of difficult, but she was a good sport and did everything she was supposed to. I sent her up to the room, and I took Slim up to his room and made sure he got in safely. Paul and Slim gave me numerous amounts of gratitude for a job well done that night. They appreciated, for once, what I represented. I tucked them in for the night as they chanted, "We're alive! We're alive!" Upon leaving, I posted two Honolulu police officers outside Slim's door for twelve hours. We all slept well because Honolulu police secured the perimeter of the hotel, the lobby, and each entertainer's floor. Thank God!!!!

It was the next day, and our problems were far from over. It was time to go, but Slim was finishing a rendezvous with Nicole from the night before. He was really pushing time because we were close to missing the flight. He continued to take his time, as usual. As he was preparing to leave, I went to talk to Sarge and Rowe (Dre's security). They told me that Dre, Snoop, Xzibit, and the rest of their crew decided to stay another day. I thought we were all flying back together, considering all the drama with Death Row, but it was cool. Or at least I thought. Slim's crew was a little disappointed that no one told them about the change of travel plans. Upon arriving at the airport, I was on the lookout for any Death Row members. I was still uneasy about the events that took place. The plane began to board, and everything was calm. We were the last ones boarding the plane, and the flight attendant made the last-call announcement. I'm thinking to myself, This is going to be a good flight! No Death Row guys in sight! Just as were buckling our seat belts and the doors were closing, I heard "Hold that door, hold that door!" Now, I was thinking, oh, shit! It can't be! Death Row was in the house, and they were thirteen deep! Immediately, I jumped out of my seat to tell Dean (Slim's A&R person) to call Jimmy Iovine at Interscope. I said, "Call Jimmy right now! Tell him to have some off-duty LAPD officers at the terminal door when we land because Death Row is on this plane! I also need a cargo van with someone to get our luggage, plus two limos, one limo as a decoy. Tell Jimmy to come through for us or we're FUCKED!!!!!" I went right to first class and alerted Paul and Slim of the situation.

Paul's reply was, "You got to be fucking kidding me!" I said, "It's real man. I've got us set up with some added security from LAPD when we land. Jimmy Iovine has already been notified, and everything is in place." Slim was already out for the count because he had taken a Valium earlier. I made my rounds and informed the whole crew. In the midst of doing my job, one the guys from Death Row tried flirting with my wife. I didn't overreact, because it may have been a ploy. I stayed focused and awake. These Death Row guys made their presence known. I was outnumbered. I remained calm. I knew they wouldn't do too much on the plane with the US Marshals regulations. If it wasn't for my quick thinking and calm reactions, there's no telling what the outcome could have been.

About four hours passed, and I was trying to relax a little bit but not too much. All I did was read my Bible, and that was the only thing I had to get me through. As soon as I put down my Bible, in came the devil. One of the Death Row guys walked past me with a couple of bottles of Hennessy in his hands. He turned toward me with a grim look, as if he knew I was with Slim. I said to myself, "OK, I can't trip. There are thirteen of them and only one of me. I'm my only backup." I was watching the guy and thought he was going to use the bathroom in first class. He was looking back at me the whole time, agitating me. He walked right by the bathroom and entered into first class where Slim was sitting. I proceeded to follow, and the Death Row guys got up and followed me. I saw the guy looking for Slim. I notified the flight attendant of the situation. She made an announcement for the group of guys who were following me to have a seat. I didn't approach the guy yet because he possibly could have known someone else in first class. Then he made a beeline right to Slim. He tapped Slim, who was asleep. I intervened, "My man, can I help you with something?" And he was like, "Naw, you can't help me with shit." I said, "Let's start over. Slim has had a long weekend, as you know. He is asleep now and is not trying to kick it about no business right now. You are up here in first class making these people uncomfortable." The guy was like, "Man, why are you tripping?" I told him, "I'm not tripping, I'm being very polite. Slim is not trying to kick it about any business right now! If you need to talk business, here is his manager, Paul Rosenberg. He handles all of his business conversations."We started to argue back and forth. By this time Slim was up, and he wanted to hear what the guy had to say. I backed up and let them talk, while watching Slim's facial expressions.

The guy was talking so low in Slim's ear that I couldn't hear what he was saying over the noise of the plane. Later on, I found out that the guy said, "Now, you know I could have jumped up on that stage the other night and fucked you up! But instead of fucking you up, I'll kick some business.You need to come on and work with me! I got some good groups, and we can help each other out. You need to leave Dre alone

The hardest working man in hip-hop.

anyway, because he's a buster!" Slim told him, "I don't appreciate you coming up here and waking me up, then bad-mouthing Dre. Plus trying to strongarm me into working with you. Man, I don't work like that!" I stepped in and said, "That's enough man! You need to go on back to your seat because you are agitating him." He was like, "Man, who the fuck are you? You don't know nothing about me!" I said,"Well, you don't know nothing about me either! But you are going to find out as soon as we get off this plane! Why don't you get back to your seat and we can all enjoy the rest of this flight. It doesn't have to be like this." He replied,"You are supposed to be Slim's bodyguard or something?" I said "Yea, that and a little bit more." The guy said, "Alright!" and went back to his seat. The people around us sensed the tension and knew that we weren't together.

Paul asked, "Was that one of the Death Row guys?" I said, "You know that was one of the Death Row guys, man, so don't even ask me that shit! You knew they were on this plane! There are thirteen of them and only one of me." I'm a strong, big fellow, but I couldn't handle them all. They had the upper hand. This is why I always stressed getting vests for us. We needed additional security. By this time, my wife sent the stewardess up to check on me before I could make it back to check on her, and I told the stewardess what was going on. She started to panic, but I reassured her that we had everything under control. I asked Dean, the A&R guy, if he was absolutely sure that Jimmy Iovine had called and set up the off-duty police officers. I asked him to have the officers in position when the plane landed. I needed to be sure because my biggest fear was that there would be more Death Row guys waiting for us at the terminal. I told Dean that a guy from Death Row had just tried to strong-arm Slim. I told everybody to be at the door as soon as the plane landed. The shit was getting serious.

I told the stewardess what was going on and that she needed to let the pilot know to make an announcement upon our exit. The deal was to let first class off first, or else there was going to be some drama going down on the plane. The flight attendant was in a state of panic. She knew about Death Row through the negative press. My people and me had our seat belts off as soon as the plane started coasting. The Death Row guys were looking around, looking like trouble. The pilot made the announcement for everyone to remain seated until first class exited the plane, using the excuse that there was a sick passenger in first class who needed to exit. I grabbed my wife's hand. There were a few passengers who had gotten wind of what was going down and were like, "Fuck that. I'm not waiting on him," you know, the typical scared-as-hell white people. I told them that they would have to get back because we were getting off the plane first. Before that door even opened all the way, we were walking off that plane, and I mean speed walking. Five off-duty police officers formed a circle around all of us and escorted us to the limo. There were two limos and a van. One limo was used as a decoy, and the van was used to get our luggage. The pilot held the passengers in for an extra five minutes to give us a head start. Paul, "Mr. Know It All About Security,Mr. Paper Gangster," looked like a punk, he was so afraid. When the police officers were taking us to the car, the first thing out of his mouth was this weak little, "Hey, what about me? Isn't anybody going to stay with me?"

Paul was just standing in the middle of the airport whining. We never broke stride, and if someone was after us, he would have been the first one hit, standing there whining because he had a connecting flight from California to New York. I don't know if anyone stayed with him; all I know is it looked like a movie, with Paul standing there looking scared shitless whimpering out, "Hey, Slim, call me, man...call me."We made it safely back to the hotel, and we were well protected on our trip back.The decoy limo left first, and we took off in the other direction, toward the hotel. Once at the hotel, we checked into another hotel under aliases, just to play it safe. My wife and I spent a sleepless night, and she was like, "Man, you have an exciting job," and I was like, "Exciting? Man, this shit is life threatening!" I didn't expect all of this. I just wanted to make some money and make some connections and get the Wadsquad off the ground, maybe get into a few skirmishes—not this. The next morning, Interscope handpicked some police officers to stand outside Slim's door, while I dropped my wife off at the airport. I was in the limo after dropping my wife off, and the limo driver told me he heard that we got into it with Death Row last night. I was like,"How do you know that?" and he was like, "People talk, man. I used to drive for Death Row." I must have had the look of fear on my face. I thought it was a setup and they had me, but I guess my mind was playing tricks on me. I said, "Damn, I didn't expect it to go down like this," and the guy said, "No, man, it's cool. I don't drive for them anymore; I used to," and he went on to tell me how he wasn't originally from California but from Brooklyn, so we kicked it, and he turned out to be OK.

But as soon as he dropped me off at the hotel, we switched hotels again because I didn't want to take any chances, and within a twenty-four-hour period, we switched hotels three times. That day, we had to meet Dre in the studio, but before we did that we met with Interscope to tell Jimmy Iovine that he was going to have to do something about this bullshit because it was way out of hand. He basically blew the whole thing off. He said, "Don't let those guys get to you. They do this all the time. You're the new kid on the block. You're a white kid, and they're going to try to come at you and intimidate you. That's just part of the game." I interjected at this point and said, "Look, Mr. Iovine, you and I have never had any words, but this man has a daughter at home, I have a family back home, and we are trying to make it back to them, but we are basically sitting out here naked. What I need you to do is to allow me to handpick some extra help, preferably some guys who are armed." Although I was certified, I was still waiting on my permits. I had pepper spray, but this was LA, and these guys eat pepper spray for lunch. So Jimmy Iovine called the Death Row guys on the phone, telling them to come up while we were sitting right there in the office.

Their lawyer called Jimmy right back, and he told their lawyer to come up to his office, as well. I was like, "Now, why did you do that? I didn't come up here to see these guys again; I just looked at them all weekend. I came up here to get some extra help, not meet with these guys." Slim and I were sitting there with no guns, no vests, just butt-ass naked. He was like, "Don't worry about it. I know how to deal with these guys." One of the street representatives from Death Row was on his way up. Slim and I quickly had to scurry to the next office over, where a gentleman named David Cohen worked, who was in charge of hiring security for various people. He was a nice guy, and we told him what happened. Since we were next door to the office where the Death Row representatives were, we couldn't talk too loudly.We were told not to leave the building until the Death Row guy had been gone at least a half hour. It was just real hectic. One thing I learned sitting in that office with Mr. Cohen was that I did not have to accept the minimal amount of money that I was making. I was able to handpick and interview the guys whom I wanted to work with me. Interscope paid these guys $45 an hour. So, here I was working with two guys, whom I chose, and while they were on twelve-hour shifts each and I was on a twenty-four-hour shift, I was making less than them. I knew for sure I was getting pimped.

I started making mental notes at that point, and I didn't have anything against these guys because Lord knows they had my back. The only thing was they were a little too old, but they had guns and were retired and off-duty police officers, so as long as their trigger fingers worked, that was fine with me.We got to the studio and told Dre what happened, and basically his attitude was, "Oh, well, welcome to the world of Death Row. You are in the bullshit now no matter what you do."We were like, "Just like that?" and he was like, "Yeah, just like that." If you mess with Dre, you inherit his beef. And with you being the bodyguard, you are the first person they would try to get. Everybody said the guy from Death Row was always starting something but wasn't going to do shit, and I was like, "Well, I don't underestimate nobody. I'm not from here."We did the studio, and I told Slim that we had to lay low that day and that he couldn't be calling all these girls up to the room because they could set us up, you never know, but do you think he listened? He dealt with at least three or four girls out in California, and they were OK for groupies, but you never know who they know. Like I said before, when it came down to beef and pussy, Slim always paid more attention to the pussy and not the beef that was going on. Later on that evening, I really started to ask myself why I was there.Why was I working for Slim Shady? I could have been an everyday Joe at home with my family working at GM instead of being out here risking my life in this crazy music industry, caught up in all this drama. I started to feel anxious and depressed. I really began to pressure Paul and Slim for a life insurance policy at this point because my life was important to me, and it was damn sure important to my family, but I knew it didn't mean shit to Slim and Paul. Finally, we worked out a deal on a life insurance policy, and that was the best thing that came of that drama.

Slim didn't take the beef seriously, as long as it wasn't in his face. I was reading everything I could get my hands on to educate myself on the West Coast culture. I read books on Death Row, gangs, Aftermath, Eazy-E – anything that could teach me something. I read about the past so that I could learn things to help me out in the present, so that I would make it to the future. What I was dealing with was way bigger than me—it was bigger than life. These cats in California don't believe in fistfighting, they are all about the gun smoke. They only care about who smokes who first. Personally, I have no interest in being caught up in the midst of any of that. I decided to call Slim and have a heart-to-heart. I say, "Look, Slim, the bottom line is we need some bulletproof vests. I have called around to several places, and they don't have vests in my size in stock. They say it's going to take three weeks to get my size in, but I don't have time to sit around in California for three weeks with no vest on." They had vests to fit Slim because he is a small guy, but I wasn't about to be unprotected while he was protected. The only place I found that had my size was in Detroit. The thing was, if Slim was wearing a vest, then I was wearing a vest, too. So I said, "Look, Paul has finally decided to get us some vests. Finally. I think you should take Jimmy Iovine up on his offer to pay for you to record somewhere else, like in New York, San Francisco, or Miami." Slim said he liked recording in LA, so he wasn't going to record at any of those other studios. This conversation caused conflict between me and Slim because I could tell by the tone of his voice that it wasn't about him liking to record out in LA, it was about him trying to prove that he was some tough little white boy who wasn't afraid of Death Row. But he was afraid, and I knew it. He was scared.

I said, "Look, man, everybody knows you can hold your own, man. But you keep in mind that dead rappers don't make any money, man. We are in over our heads here. We are sitting in the lion's den. We need to go home and let this cool off for a couple of days. Paul has finally agreed to pay for the vests, and I am going home to get us some vests and try to bring a gun back. You can stay here if you want to. I am going home because that is the only place I can find my size vest right now." He took this like I just wanted to go home and see my family, so the conversation got on a personal level at this point. I said, "Look, man, don't hate me because my home situation is better than yours. You need to go home and handle that problem, anyway. I can't help it if my wife and kids want to and love to see me. Don't be mad because my wife doesn't tell me I have to stay in a hotel and that she doesn't tell me that I can't even drive the car that I bought. My family loves to see me, so of course I am going to see them when I go home, but I am going to get us some vests, and I will be right back out." I said I would try to bring a gun, but it would be

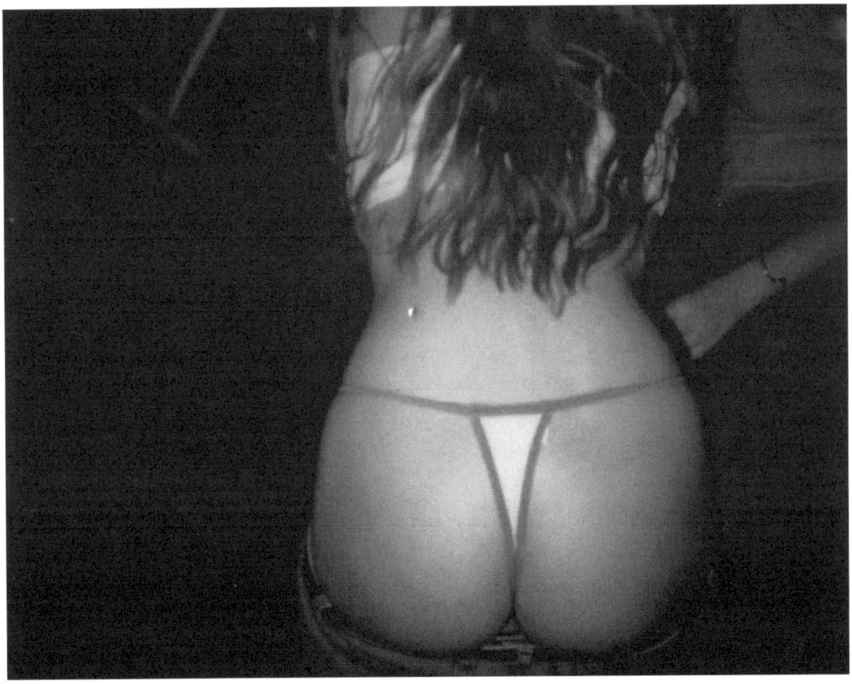

Arizona girls drop it like it's hot!

difficult to do so since airport security knew whom I was affiliated with and had started to do random searches on me.

I told him I wasn't going to jeopardize my future and my life trying to smuggle an illegal gun in, though. Unfortunately, I wasn't able to bring back a weapon, but while I was gone, I arranged for an armed off-duty police officer whom we had worked with before to stay with Slim. The officer and I worked something out that when I came back he would have a 9 mm and a 12-gauge shotgun pump for me. At home, I had already made arrangements with Paul and Slim's accountant to pay for the vests and all the hardware that came with them, like the batons and the pepper spray. I had the place I was purchasing the equipment from hold everything for me so that it would be a quick process, because I only had two days. I got to the place to pick up the equipment, and Paul hadn't done one thing he was supposed to have done. All he had to do was fax the guy over the credit card number to pay for the equipment, but he didn't. I went to the place with no knowledge of this and ended up wasting my time. I tried via every form of communication possible to contact Paul, but he never returned my messages. I had to go over his head and get authorization from the accountant's assistant in order to get the equipment paid for. Later that day I got a call from Paul, and he was all pissed off because I went over his head, and I told him I did it because he wouldn't respond to any of my messages, and if he would have done what he was supposed to do in the first place, none of this would have been necessary.

Having to wait on Paul caused me to have to stay home another day. All Slim saw was that I took an extra day to be with my family, and he accused me of running from the Death Row situation. I said, "Look man, first of all, yes I spent time with my family, but my staying over was Paul's fault for not taking care of his business the way he was supposed to. Second of all, I don't have to try to prove that I'm a tough guy, that's you trying to prove that. If I was going to run from Death Row, I would have busted the fuck up in Hawaii. I don't believe you have the nerve to say that shit to me while I am always fighting your battles and knocking muthafuckas out, dislocating my shoulder protecting you! I don't have to prove I'm a tough guy.Tough guys are dead men. Only the smart guys live."

Back in LA, with our equipment, I felt safe. I wasn't on no vigilante shit, I was on some survival shit, that's the attitude I had being back out there. I felt like leaving my house, leaving from Detroit to California, I was going back to war. I knew that if I slipped or if Slim slipped, our lives would be in jeopardy. I tried to instill this in Slim's mind, and he would wear the vest most of the time and only take it off when he got hot in the recording studio, but that only lasted a short time. I wore my vest from the time I woke up to the time I went to sleep. One time, I even fell asleep in my vest because I was on some paranoid shit. I would sit outside the studio door for the sixteen-hour sessions while Slim was recording with Dre. I wore my bulletproof vest, my baton, my pepper spray, and my 20-shot Glock on my lap at all times. I placed my off-duty police officers at each exit, with guns ready just in case any gangsters showed.They already knew to shoot to kill. I was on a survival mission to make it home to my family in one piece.

Right around this time, I got some unpleasant news. Sarge and Rowe, Dre's security guards, had been fired. My mind was blown. They were my mentors, the best bodyguards I had ever known, and they had really taken good care of Dre.They had been fired? They took care of Dre, but Dre fired them. I thought that was pretty fucked up.The rumor was that they asked for more money and had been fired and told that there was no room for what they were making in the budget.The most shocking part for me was that they replaced Sarge and Rowe with former bodyguards of Death Row. I knew if the best in the business had been fired, supposedly for asking for more money, then Slim and Paul would get it in their minds that if Dre wasn't paying his security guys more money, why should they? I knew that Paul would start tripping, and that is exactly what happened.

The thing that bothered me was that these guys used to work for Death Row. I think I was more worried about these guys than anybody else.Why would Aftermath hire the same guys that used to work for Mr. Marion Knight? Unless they had established a bond with Dre before and weren't really affiliated with the bullshit when Dre left Death Row, I couldn't understand it. When I think of Death Row, I immediately put my defenses up. I immediately acquainted myself with these guys, and they seemed pretty cool, but the first thing out of their mouths was, "We used to work for Death Row, we used to be Suge Knight's bodyguards," so a flag went up that I was going to have to watch these cats. However, in retrospect I doubt if Dre would allow his company to hire someone who would put his life in danger. It was weird because the guys asked me to let them bring some additional guys on to help me, but I was like, "Naw, man, I'm gonna stick with my own people, people that I hand-picked myself. No offense to y'all." I acquainted myself with these guys, but at the same time I kept myself at a distance because I was just really leery of anyone who was outside of our camp for the most part. Needless to say, those guys did their job. They kept the studio on lock-down, but they just weren't Sarge and Rowe. I wasn't entirely comfortable in that environment without Sarge and Rowe.

I considered these guys to be the best in the game. But then, we were all dispensable. The worse part of it all was that Sarge and Rowe found out that they were fired through me. The day they were fired, we were in the studio, and I received a call that they were fired. I couldn't contact them that weekend because they had been given that weekend off. It turned out they were fired on their day off! It was truly a mess, because when Rowe got the message I left him, he called me. I didn't say on the message that he was fired, I said I was sorry about the news. When he returned my call, he was like, "Man, what were you talking about, what news?" I then told him what happened.We were at the studio right then, and there were two new cats from Death Row working their spots. Rowe told Sarge the news, and to this day they have no idea why they were dismissed. Aftermath never gave them a formal dismissmal. All they knew were the rumors that they had asked for too much money. Personally, I can't see those guys asking for too much money. Everybody needs a raise here and there.They had been with Dre at least a couple of years.You put your life on the line for these people, and you are the least appreciated soul in the camp. Somewhere down the line, someone has to realize that you can't do your personal security like that. I am speaking for Sarge and Rowe, myself, and all of the other guys out here who refuse to get pimped in the security game. The worse part was that I didn't have the security of having Sarge and Rowe there. If some gangsters decided to run up in the studio and start some shit, I knew Sarge and Rowe had my back. I had my other guys there, but again, they weren't Sarge and Rowe. I talk to them every now and then, and they are doing pretty good. Because they are the best, they are always going to have work. It was just reinforced to me through their experience that you can put your life on the line for your client, but you are still disposable.

More Trouble Brewing

I was enjoying my day at home – doing some dishes, calling everybody and telling them I was home – and it felt good to call everybody and give them the lowdown on all the shit that had been going down. Everybody was just on edge and couldn't wait to hear what happened next, who I had seen and who I was hanging out with in the studio, and for me that's never really been any big deal because I've always done security for different people and had pretty much met everybody; they are just people with money, ya know? So, I caught up with my people, and we all hooked up and tried to get some things going. It was just cool, and I really enjoyed my first day home. On October 16th I called Slim, with like, "Yo, man, whass up? What's the deal?" and he said."Well, yo, man, tonight we all want to hang out, so I'm going to give you a call and tell you what's what so we can all hang out, man. I want to go to The Shelter (an underground hip-hop club in Detroit where Slim Shady paid a lot of his dues). So, I was like, "OK, cool.We can do that. Just hit me when you're ready."

On that day, I took my son to get his hair cut and went and washed the grip again, did a little shopping, and took the wife to the movies.While I was at the movies I got a call from Slim telling me what time we were hanging out, so I was like, "That's all right, that's cool, man. I'll see you in a couple hours." I told the old lady what was going on, and she kind of understood that I was on call, but she didn't like it at all and cursed me out because I left my phone on in the show. Even though I had it on low ring, she still didn't like it, and she was like,"Well, when you are with me, you shouldn't have it on at all," and I was like, "Well, baby, you know that even when I'm at home, this is my job. I told you that before, and I need you to be supportive of that." She felt like Slim was robbing her of her time with me, and I can understand that, but at the same time this was my job, and I needed her to be supportive. I guess at that time she felt like she was being more than supportive, and we got into a blowout about that, but it blew over, we resolved it, and it was cool. As the night went on, Slim never called me back, but I got a call from Proof telling me that they had all gone out, and they were deep enough so that they didn't need me, and I was like, "All right, that's cool." It was cool that the D12 had got together to take Slim out and get him out of that hotel room, because that's no way for anybody to have to spend their birthday—you know, alone, beefing with your old lady, and you can't see your kids.You need to be around somebody because that's some suicidal shit there. But again, as usual, Proof saved the day—that's my man.

October 17th was Slim's birthday, and his crew took him out the night before because he wanted to spend the day of his birthday with Hailey. I called him to see if he needed anything or if he wanted me to go out anywhere with him and also to wish him a happy birthday. He said,"Na, I'm just going to chill with the family. I'm cool." I said, "OK, man. If you need anything just call me and let me know, it's all good." I proceeded to have a good day that day. I went to church and went to go visit some of my family. It was cool. I had slipped back into family mode, doing my church duties and visiting my family and friends, and it was beautiful. It was a complete day; it looked like I might actually enjoy two days in a row off this time. I can say even though I didn't get paid the amount of money I would have liked to have been paid, the downtime of the job with the pay was the best damn part. But the thing is that with that came the inconveniences, as well. But other than that, it was OK.

But as the day came to an end, I was sitting in my fully furnished basement, where I always dwell when I am at home on the Internet. It was about 10 p.m., and I got a call from Paul Rosenburg, Slim's manager. I knew it was some deep shit because the only time Paul calls me is if there is something very important or if something very fucked up has happened. I was thinking it was one of two things: either something was wrong with Slim or we had to leave tomorrow. So I was like, "What's up, man? Everything straight?" And he was like, "Naw, man. I got some bad news." I was thinking we had to leave tomorrow, so I'm like, "Yeah, man. Well, what's up?" And he was like,"Kurupt's bodyguard got killed last night, and Daz got grazed in the leg." I was like, "What?" and he said another guy got shot, and I asked him whom they were saying did it, and he said, "I don't know.They got a good idea, but they don't really know. There were allegations about the beef between Kurupt and the Ruff Ryders with the shit he said on a song. Then there was another rumor that it was gang related." But the one thing I did know was that it was a bodyguard dead. And what was so coincidental was that it happened at one of the studios we had been at once or twice. This was too close to home. The sad thing was that this guy was supposedly a family man who had two kids. It was truly sad, whether he was a family man or not. Hearing about somebody else being killed made me look back to the situation in Hawaii and the situation at the studio.

That was one of my biggest fears, what happened to that bodyguard. I often worried about somebody running up in the studio shooting to kill somebody. Some guys who had nothing to do with us but had beef with us because Slim was white, a rapper, and the newest member of Aftermath. Unfortunately it had became a reality for someone; fortunately, not me. I had met the guy once at a video shoot, and it really hit home for me. It was depressing. That could have been me!? He was a soldier, a bodyguard, a fellow brother in this business. He was down for his client, now he was done. Death. At any given time this could happen to anybody. My goal was to learn more about the situation. I didn't want to be drawing any conclusions or pointing the finger at anybody. I knew something like this was going to happen.

The heat was so thick out there, with shit going on in California, I knew it would only be a matter of time before something like that would happen. I'm just glad we had been out of there in enough time. I said, "Paul, you know what? We should not do any more recording out there, man! This should be the last sign to remind you guys how unsafe it is out there recording." Some fellow bodyguards out in LA told me the shooting happened at about 11:30 p.m. Kurupt's bodyguard was the first to get shot. I guess there were some guys in the parking lot who were trying to come into the studio, and the bodyguards wouldn't let them in. Unfortunately, the bodyguard wasn't wearing a vest, and they shot him five times in his upper body. They killed him—he died right there in the parking lot. Supposedly, a second bodyguard or another person was present and pushed a pop machine against the door as a barricade to keep the guys from coming in.

Before all that happened, there were at least two more people who got shot. Another person got shot a couple of times, and supposedly Daz got grazed in his leg. I was like, Damn, I can't believe this. I go look at MTV news online, and lo and behold it's telling the story just like that. And I was shaken up by it, you know? I started looking at my situation once again. Every time I reflected on my situation, I looked deeper than the last. And I'm thinking, This shit is getting too damn serious, it's getting too damn deep. I mean, you can't even prepare for something like that. You can be so totally prepared and people can still catch you off guard—it just goes to show you.

Paul and I decided after talking at that time,"Hey, let's call Slim and let him know," and Paul was like,"Yeah, he doesn't know yet. Let's call him right now, so we can catch up with Slim and let him know what's going on." When we called Slim, he was like, "Damn! Are you serious?" and we were like, "Yep, Kurupt's bodyguard is dead, man.Three people have been shot, with one dead, in California. And we just left. Remember, I was telling you, man; it was a matter of time. The bodyguard wasn't wearing a vest." I said, "Man, on the real, we shouldn't go back out there and do any recording." I said, "Man, they're on some different shit out there, man.We cannot fuck with them cats. Let them do their thing.We've got many studios right here in Detroit.There are a lot of people who fly from all over to come here and record.Ya know, shit, just record here, man." And for the first time, and one of the only times, all three of us agreed—we agreed to the studio time being done in Detroit. If there was anything Dre had to do, he would have to send the reels up, and if there was a vocal part for Dre, they spoke about flying Dre in. And I'm thinking,Wow. Okay, finally we're all on the same page. I'm also thinking, Ya know, it's sad to have to have a bodyguard die to get them on the same page with me because every revelation I have given them about this nonsense that had been going on had come to pass. And finally I'm like the best thing since fried chicken. Now, I know what I'm talking about. I always knew what I was talking about. Unfortunately, someone had to pass away for him to understand that or even respect what was going on.

I got off the phone with them and called Rowe, Dre's ex-bodyguard out in California, and was like, "Yo, what is going on, man? Paul just called and told me that Kurupt's bodyguard has been killed," and he was like, "Yeah, man, I heard. I'm trying to find out if it's my boy because he had two bodyguards that he used." I said,"Well, they said this guy's name was Dwayne." And Rowe said, "Well, naw that ain't my partner, man, but I'm going to call you back." So, he got some information and called me back, and he was like, "Ya, man, this is the part of the game we go through that cats don't understand; our life is on the line every day. Anytime could be your last moment." And I told him how me, Slim, and Paul actually agreed to continue recording here in Detroit, and that if they needed Dre to do something they would fly him or his reels in, and that would be the best thing to do. Rowe got a kick out of that and was like, "You know, that's a damn shame that a man had to die for them to respect and understand how severe this shit is." And I said, "You know what, Rowe? That's the same thing I'm saying."We kicked it for a little bit on the phone, and when we got off the phone, I sat and prayed for my man and his family.

By this time it was pretty late, and I went upstairs and looked in my elder son's room and stared at him while he was asleep, just realizing how blessed I am and thinking about my man's situation who is gone now. He'll never be able to look at his kids again. And I was just really realizing how blessed I am and just appreciating every moment I have. After I looked at my older boy, I tucked him in and gave him a kiss on the forehead and told him that I loved him and I was glad to be home, and I said that with a tear in my eye. It really hurt, you know, to see somebody die in the line of duty like that and realize that could have been you. After I tucked my son in, I went in my room, where my wife and baby boy were. At this time, he was about seven or eight months old. I had been on the road so long I couldn't even remember my son's exact age at the time. Anyway, they were sleeping peacefully. I'm looking at them, and as my baby was sleeping, he had kind of a little smile on his face; I guess he was dreaming about little angels—and that moment was a heavenly moment. My son's smile meant to me that everything was going to be all right as long as I kept God in my corner. I look back now and reflect on Psalm 1:24.Verses two and three say it best: "If it had not been for the Lord who was on our side, when men rose up against us they would have swallowed us alive when their wrath was kindled against us."

Monday, October 18th

I got a call from Paul around noon regarding the early departure. Instead of us leaving that Friday before we had to do "Saturday Night Live," he wanted us to leave that Wednesday. And I was like, "Man, you know what? I'm not leaving Wednesday. I'm leaving Saturday. I've already talked to Rock and Noel, and they said they would cover for me." Paul agreed to that arrangement, so it was cool. I wanted to stay in Detroit longer because I had a lot of loose ends I had to tie up and had to get my family situation together.The home life was cool, but the marriage was still suffering. Trying to make up for months in a matter of days just can't be done.

Later on that evening, the wife and I got into a big-ass blowout, probably the biggest dispute we've ever had. The first thing I did, which was during the midst of the argument, was call Paul and tell him that I changed my mind and had decided to come out on Wednesday with Slim, so to get me a ticket. He said, "Are you sure?" And I said, "Yeah, definitely get a ticket for me. I'm positive I'm not going to wait until Saturday. I'm coming out Wednesday. There are a lot of things going on at the home front, and I need to get away." Basically, hell was about to erupt at that point because I was frustrated, and she was frustrated. I wondered whether this road or this music thing was pulling my life apart—was I changing, was she changing, what was going on, and what was the deal?

One of my wife's biggest points was that I wasn't helping around the house. I was like, "What the fuck do you mean I'm not helping? I'm away on the road. I send my entire money home, I'm getting home improvements made, and I'm paying all the bills.When I come home, I've done my work—there's nothing else for me to do. So, don't nag me about doing anything because I am doing my part." She would say, "Well, you could at least help wash some dishes, etc.," and I can honestly admit I probably was on an ego trip because I felt like I was paying the bills, I was the head of the household, and that I didn't have to do any more than what I was doing. I felt like I wasn't out playing, I was out working, and I was paying all the bills, everything was taken care of. I can honestly say that was selfish on my part.Time tends to heal all wounds though, and it was only a matter of days before I was scheduled to go back out on the road. It was strange because when I was away I couldn't wait to get home, and once I was home for a couple of days, I couldn't wait to get back on the road.

It was Tuesday, and I was supposed to leave Wednesday, so I had a lot to do that day. I ended up changing my flight to that Saturday to spend quality time with my family, and that was the best decision I've ever made.

I was home playing with my sons, and we were having fun. I was looking at my baby boy's christening pictures, which I had missed. I noticed how much he had grown from two months to nine months. He had teeth coming in, he had gotten bigger, and he was starting to try to say some words. I was trying to remember the months in between two and nine months of his life, and I couldn't. It really started to bother me. Fortunately, my wife and mother-in-law, two good, supportive women, took a lot of pictures in my absence to keep me abreast of how he was growing. Therefore, I was able to take part in his growth vicariously. A picture may be worth a thousand words but there is nothing like being there. I missed all that. I sacrificed so much to help make Slim successful, and he didn't appreciate it at all. One day when Slim grows up, he'll understand.

5

EUROPEAN TURMOIL

A few days passed, and I was all packed up, ready to leave for at least a month. My wife and kids dropped me off at the airport. That was always the saddest part because I could envision my wife and kids watching me until I disappeared into the crowd.

My first stop was New York, where I met up with Slim, Paul, DJ Head, Proof, Rock, and Noel. We had "Saturday Night Live" to do that night, and Dre and Snoop were going to perform "Still Got Love for the Streets," and Slim and Dre were going to perform "Forgot About Dre." This is where the serious bullshit began. I got to New York, and I was pissed because I had to catch a cab. It was mad hectic out there. I couldn't catch up with anyone to find out what hotel to go to, and there I was in the cab with the meter running. Finally, Mark called me back with the information. Once again, Paul hadn't handled his business properly. The room was paid for, but they wanted me to pay ahead for incidentals. They wanted me to leave a deposit on the bar. I had to call Paul and wait for him or Mark to call me back to get that taken care of. This day was off to a bad start already. Finally, I got to the room. I hooked up with Rock and Noel from J&A Security, who covered for me on my days off. They told me Slim didn't want to get out of bed. "Why didn't y'all get him out of bed?" Slim claimed he was too tired to work. He was blowing off a $10,000 photo shoot that the label had already paid in full. I called Mark and told him, "It seems like y'all can't get shit done unless I am here. What's the deal?"

Mark said he was in the studio for seventeen hours last night, and they didn't get in until seven this morning. That's how it was all the time in California. I'm used to that. Slim said, "Fuck the photo shoot, and fuck the magazine!" He was tired, plus he had his mistress, Kessia, with him. I said, "Well, he is the boss, so let him do what he wants to do. Y'all are going to learn that if he doesn't want to do something, then leave him be. If he wants to let the record company recoup ten grand because he missed the shoot, then that's his business." Mark asked if I could convince him to get ready. "I'll do it, but y'all shouldn't have scheduled that shit so close together. That is the difference between you and me. When we were in California, I knew that after an all-night session in the studio, nothing was going to happen the next morning. You should know better than to schedule something for Slim before three in the afternoon. The man is tired. Let him rest. He has to do Saturday Night Live tonight and everything. I'm not fucking with him!"

Slim blew off the photo shoot, and I went to get him together at four in the afternoon. Slim was like, "Yo, what's up, Naz? Do you believe this shit? They scheduled this photo shoot all early, and, shit, Paul has been calling up here talking all that shit, man. I need my sleep, man!" That was one of the biggest things in Slim's little world. The first was Hailey, and second was his sleep. Then make sure you got his Vicodin, his E, his Bacardi, his Burger King, and his Taco Bell. Oh, and some fresh gear, which Mark always provided for him. Oh, and Niketown! Nothing else existed to him. Slim was running his mouth about how Mark and Paul were talking shit to him about his not getting up to do the photo shoot. Slim was in the studio all night doing a song for Royce Da 5'9"'s album. I told Slim, "Well they fucked up, man. They should know by now that you need to get your sleep." I turned on Slim's shower like, "Come on, man. We got to make this move, we got to bounce." By this time Kessia was up, and she was telling me how long they were in the studio. I told her it was like that every day in California. I said they should know better than this because he needs at least ten hours of sleep—at least.

We all headed out, and by this time word got out that Slim Shady was staying at this hotel, and there was a shitload of groupies out front. Unfortunately, that was the only exit we could take. Slim signed a few autographs. We all loaded up in the limo and Yukon Denali and headed to the venue where they film Saturday Night Live. The Saturday Night

Live staff told us no smoking weed in the dressing rooms. Everybody agreed until Snoop and Dre came through with the "sticky icky." We got it all on tape, with Snoop showing everybody how to smoke weed. Snoop would inhale it, exhale it out his nose, then suck it back in through his mouth – it was amazing. I had never seen any shit like that before. We were there eight hours because we had to film the show in its entirety as a practice run, then do the show live.

Security was extra tight, due to what had recently happened to Kurupt's bodyguard. We didn't know whether it was an East Coast beef or gang related, we just wanted to take the extra measures to make sure that everyone was safe. The show went smoothly, and they all rocked it, and we went back and chilled at the hotel. It was at this point that Slim's staff found out Paul and Slim would be taking a separate flight. Jimmy Iovine arranged for the two of them to catch $10,000 flights. This was how Paul decided to spend Slim's bonus from Interscope. Slim had earned this bonus from performing on Saturday Night Live. They would fly on Concord jets from New York to London. Those flights are usually seven or eight hours, but on a Concord jet it could be reduced to an hour. The rest of us were like, "Why didn't he take the twenty grand and share it among the crew instead of spending it on the plane ride that would get them there quicker for no reason?" Plus, I was supposed to be his bodyguard, so why was I not going with Slim? Eventually, Slim was going to find himself alone. Paul may have been a big guy, but if some shit went down all he could do was call a criminal lawyer.

Slim and Paul left at 5:30 a.m. on October 25th, and this was the beginning of the European tour. I call it the "European turmoil" because nothing went the way it was planned. One of the biggest complaints from everyone was that Slim had spent seven grand on Kessia's plane ticket. He made sure she flew first class from Florida to New York, then first class from New York to London, and everywhere else with us around Europe. The crew really felt like that was a slap in the face. It was an insult. It basically added insult to injury. Flights in Europe are already small. I was crammed next to an old lady who refused to give me the aisle seat. She wanted to be able to talk to her sister during the flight. Her feet weren't even touching the ground. She had to be all of four foot nothing. I was like, Oh shit, here we go. I squeezed into my seat, and I thought to myself that this old lady better not even think of the armrest. I was going to bogart the armrest, at least I was running that shit.

That's how I got back at her. I was all balled up, and this old lady was sitting there swinging her feet. We were all uncomfortable. DJ Head is a big guy, too, and he was cramped, as well. I was pissed because

Slim's mistress was in first class, comfortable and eating the finest foods, and we were cramped up eating leftover refrozen shit! We were pissed because he spent $7,000 flying some female out, but he couldn't even take care of us. When we ask for a raise of $100 or $200 a week, we can't get it.Where are your priorities? We are showing you loyalty so show us some respect on the financial end.We found out about the amount of money that Slim was paying for Kessia to fly to Europe from Paul when we were in Hawaii. Paul was bragging to Proof and I that Slim was flying Kessia out to Europe.We were like, "Cool." Then Paul said he was spending seven grand to do it. Paul said, "Yeah, Slim's big-balling now, he's spending seven grand to fly this girl out." Proof was like, "What the fuck! I can't even get a raise, and he is spending seven grand on this girl? Y'all always act like y'all don't have any money, yet you can fly her out like this!" Paul tried to laugh it off and said to Proof that they spent money on him and never asked to be repaid. Proof was like, "That's not the point! He has a bodyguard that you fly out in coach, and he is the biggest thing on the plane! You can't even put him in business class or get him a bulkhead seat, but you have her in first class! That's not right!" I said, "I know it's not right, but that's just how they do it, man." That really put us at the back of the bus. Proof went off, and Paul didn't like that. Proof worked hard, and he was the positive vibe for everybody. He kept everyone mentally together. He took care of Slim as far as making sure all the shows' formats were tight, and all he wanted was a little respect for everybody. To see Slim throwing around seven grand like that, it made us see things differently.

When I dislocated my shoulder protecting Slim, he promised me some help financially. Paul declined that, and I asked if I could have an advance from the next tour. I should have been completely compensated, as if I were still working. Proof was going through some financial hardships because when they weren't touring they weren't getting paid. Proof asked for an advance, but it took them two weeks to get it to him. Slim and Paul showed where their loyalty was.We knew where our loyalty was, but we weren't sure about them anymore. It was like a slap in the face for us.We had nothing against Kessia, but we wondered, where do we fit in? Why do we have to get treated like shit? That made us feels like third-class citizens. It reminded us where we stood when we made Slim the VIP that he is. It left a salty taste in our mouths, and we weren't going to eat that anymore. It started the tour off on the wrong foot, as well.

Finally, after three crappy-ass flights, we arrived in Oslo, a small spot in Germany. Everybody reflected on what had just happened, from the first-class thing to the Concord jets, and we all felt like we were at the bottom of the barrel. In our downtime that is what we talked about. We were like, "Damn. We have from the 25th of October to the 17th of November to deal with this Europe shit." I wasn't feeling Europe at all this second time around, especially with three weeks of bad water and pork, which none of us ate. The food was totally different, and European people from time to time tend to act a little weird. We were trying to adjust. I was like, Damn, I'm on the other side of the world, and my wife and kids are at home.

I hoped that nothing happened back home like it did the last time I was in Europe. The last time I was in Europe, my wife was in an automobile accident. She was sitting at a traffic light and this guy came along and broadsided her. She had to go to the doctor, and thank God she wasn't hurt. I was in Europe and had no way of finding out if anything did happen. Luckily, I checked my voice mail that day, and she left a message letting me know what happened. At the same time this happened, my wife's sister went into the hospital. Plus, her mother was scheduled to have an operation. I knew my wife was under a lot of stress and pressure. It was a mess, and I felt like I needed to be home. I knew if I went home I would feel like I should be on the road. I had a lot of things on my mind, as well, and I felt useless and worthless. I had some soulsearching to do because it was no longer clear to me where I stood.

Oslo was no big deal show-wise, other than throwing one guy off the stage and out the door. That was the first time a crowd ever cheered for me when I threw someone out, and they went nuts after I put a move on my man. It was cool. But no one was prepared for the next day. It was October 26th, in Stockholm. Let me give you a little history on Stockholm, Sweden. The last time we were in Stockholm, there was a lot of drama. The first time we went there was in August of 1999 for a promo tour. During that time, Slim met this young lady, and she was tight. No doubt she was tight. In fact, all the women I saw there were tight. It was like they came off an assembly line or something—tall, blond, big boobs, nice body, and nice personality. And there were some fine black women there, too. I got a chance to meet the girls from Lou Bega's group ("Mambo No. 5") and, my goodness; they were gorgeous, absolutely beautiful. On the August tour, when we arrived at the hotel, the lobby was swamped with nothing but girls ranging in age from fourteen to nineteen, all tugging on our clothes and wanting kisses, hugs, and photos. We loved it because it was all girls. We had to get help from hotel security because we couldn't even make it to the elevator. These girls were young, but were tall and looked at least five years older than they actually were. The fact that they were young didn't matter to Slim. He hooked up with this one young lady who was tight, named Agnes.

She was young, but Slim didn't know it at the time. Agnes was built like a brick house for a white girl. I have to admit, she was also very smart. This girl had her game down. She had somehow put together a fake passport. I told her before she talked to Slim I would need to see some ID because they lock people in jail in foreign countries. Everything looked legit, but I found out she used one of her friend's information and took the picture and hooked up the ID to look real. Apparently, she was able to get into bars and shit like that. One thing you have to realize is that in the States eighteen is the legal age, but in Sweden sixteen is the legal age, and in some places in Europe, fifteen is the legal age. This girl looked every bit of twenty-two. She had a fucking body! She was hot, and she was pushing up on Slim pretty tough. Slim was like, "Why don't you come up to my room?" and we checked her ID, which said she was nineteen years old. She was all over him. I left them, and they went up to his room, and a couple of hours later he came back down. Slim was hype, "Yo, man, that was the best fuck I ever had in my life. She came like eleven times." I said, "Man, she ain't come no damn eleven times!" Slim said, "Man, you should see my sheets, they are soaked! She sucked my dick, we sixty-nined. Man, she knows how to fuck!" He was totally blown away by this girl, but at the time he didn't know her real age—none of us did—she had fooled all of us. Her game was tight, so tight that Slim wanted to fly her out for the rest of that tour.However, when we went to get her a ticket, the authorities discovered that she was underage—only fifteen years old!

Lo and behold, on the second trip Slim wanted to hook up with her again. He didn't care about her age because her pussy was so tight. I had to remind him of all the drama, when her mom had the authorities threaten to come get Agnes. I told him we all could have gone to jail. Luckily, we found out what was going on, and we sent her back on the first thing that was running on gas.We called her mom and apologized because we didn't know she was only fifteen, and we told her about the fake ID and that she looked nineteen. But that didn't matter to Slim because he lived up to the lyrics of his song when basically he said, "she's fifteen, he doesn't care. Look at her bush, does she have hair? Fuck her right there on the spot, there." He lived up to his song lyrics. Whether he realized he did this or not, he did it.

More European Turmoil

We were back in Stockholm, Sweden, the land of pretty woman and underage groupies. Upon arriving at the hotel, we were welcomed by Slim Shady's fifteen-year-old mistress, Agnes. Apparently, her jealous

Slim poses with Scary Spice and Baby Spice.

friends informed her mother that she had sex with Slim Shady and was leaving the country on his tour. Her mother called our hotel forbidding Agnes to leave. Then she contacted the police and told them about Slim's involvement with an underage girl. However, Agnes disobeyed her mom and attempted travel anyway. The Interscope international representative advised Slim that he could be brought up on charges for dealing with this minor.

In some countries, a fifteen-year-old is legal—but with parental approval. Agnes' mom didn't approve at all. Slim still invited Agnes to travel with the tour. He went as far as having Agnes ride with us to the airport. We were notified by phone from the authorities that the mother wouldn't press charges if Agnes didn't attempt to leave. But if she tried to board the plane, we would all be arrested for accomplice to statutory rape! Slim's entire staff practically begged him to be wise and avoid Agnes. Slim temporarily agreed and sent her home in a taxi. However, when we returned to Stockholm, Slim continued to mess around with this girl. I had this gut feeling there were going to be some problems that night. Slim never would listen; he truly doesn't GIVE A FUCK! As

MC Proof and Paul drunk on absinthe in London, England.

soon as Slim saw Agnes, he forgot about Kessia. They were like two dogs in heat when their eyes met again. Agnes thrust her tongue in Slim's mouth, and then they hurried to a nearby restroom for a quickie. Proof was joking with some young ladies while Slim and Agnes were in the bathroom possibly getting busy. Again, I warned Slim about Agnes' age and the consequences that could follow. Mark Labelle saw Proof laughing with the young ladies and thought that would be a good time to be introduced and try to impress the ladies. Proof left the ladies and then went back to the dressing room.

Later on after the show, one of the young ladies approached Proof with some information. Apparently, Mark had made negative remarks about Proof.The young lady claimed that Mark belittled Proof in his effort to try and impress her. She said that Mark stated, "She shouldn't waste her time trying to talk to Proof because that nigger just works in the plant. He really didn't have anything to offer." This got back to Proof, and he didn't like that at all, especially since he had no interest in the lady. Proof questioned Mark, "Mark why would you say that about me to these girls that neither one of us even know? We don't know these hos, so why are you trying to impress them by putting me down?" To make it worse, Proof didn't even work at the plant. I did, so I kind of felt put into the situation like all black people work at the plant—besides the fact that he used the word "nigger." Now that term was used loosely because you heard Mark calling Jews niggers and whites niggers, but me personally I didn't call anybody that, and I didn't appreciate it at all.

I heard secondhand what Mark said about Proof from the young lady, but how true was it? I didn't know. This was the second day of the tour. Everybody was stressed out because Slim was messing around with this young girl again. Although we were in a foreign country, she was still too young for him to be dealing with, but he chose to do so. We had a long road ahead of us because the tour was scheduled for three weeks. Nobody really wanted to be there, but hey, we were making some money. That was about the best thing going. By the time Proof got this information, everybody was drunk and high from Ecstacy, weed, Martell, and Hennessy. The emotions were running high, and everyone was feeling good. Proof was telling Slim that he needed to talk to him, and Mark caught wind of what was going on. Mark was trying to get Slim's attention away from Proof. Proof then pulled Slim into a private room to talk to him about Mark's alleged racial statements. He also told him about Mark putting him down in front of a groupie.

Mark was cock-blocking and hating. Proof had reached a point where he was feeling underappreciated for all the sacrifices he had made. Proof and I had a lot in common, like leaving a child and girlfriend to help Slim's career. Proof felt disrespected as an artist and as a hype man. Proof basically built Slim's whole show. Proof had reached his threshold, and Mark's comments really set him off. I believe that if Proof hadn't controlled himself, he would have given Mark some PA treatment (Puritan Ave.). Proof hadn't come all this way for that—he tried successfully to keep his focus and his mind-set together.

I don't think Mark realized that he had stepped on Proof's toes, but he did. One thing I learned on this tour is that New York cats and Detroit cats are two totally different types of people. They handle things in two different ways. What you do to cats in New York, you can't do to cats in Detroit. We aren't going for it. We will let you know when shit is offensive to us. That's basically what went down. Proof told Slim what was said. They were all drunk and high to the extreme. I went to the restroom. Paul and Mark were in the hallway trying to figure out what Proof and Slim were discussing. I overheard Mark trying to get Slim's attention, but he wanted to get Proof out of the room. Proof told Mark to wait because he was talking to Slim. Mark said, "This is more important than what you're talking about man. I need Slim out here right now!" I guess with Mark being Slim's road manager, he was trying to use that as an edge to get Slim away from Proof, and he was just trying to keep Slim from finding out what was said earlier.

Proof preferred to tell Slim and let Slim handle the situation rather than take it into his own hands. Clearly, Mark was getting increasingly agitated and impatient. Finally, Slim told Mark that he would have to wait while he talked to Proof. Mark yelled, "Man, get dat mutha fucka outta your ear!" over and over. Proof told Slim what exactly was said. Now, Slim's drunk, Mark's drunk, and Proof seemed sober to me. I'm still in the bathroom taking a leak. The next thing I heard was a loud-ass "thump!" I mean a loud-ass Batman slap, like POW!! I didn't know what happened. I thought some groupie guys had come backstage and started some mess. I damn near zipped my business up in the zipper and ran out into the hallway to see what happened. All I saw was Paul holding Mark and Proof holding Slim. Slim had punched Mark Labelle right in his eye—BAM!!! Slim knocked the hell out of Mark.

Mark and Slim were trying to get at each other. I picked Slim up, who started trying to get physical with me. I carried him into the dressing room and slammed him on the couch. I told him to calm the fuck down. Mark remained in the hallway. Slim told me that Mark's racist remark really struck a nerve with him. No one was thinking clearly due to the liquor and drug use. He reasoned that punching Mark stemmed from being tired of all the racism that he had been faced with all his life. Actually, Slim was just using that as an excuse because he had wanted

Paul is denying Mark a raise. Mark is pleading his case.

to hit Mark for a long time. He hadn't cared too much for Mark since he came into the picture. One time, Slim wanted to fight Mark because he had taken one of his Vicodin pills. Mark was almost fired that day for ingesting Slim's drugs. Slim often felt that Mark was treating him like a little kid. However, Slim's behavior often inspired that form of treatment. Mark is the type of guy who will take care of you as long as you show him some respect, and he likes to be praised publicly.

I felt sorry for Mark at that point because he always went out of his way to take care of Slim. For example, when we would go to a foreign country or out of state, Mark would literally go out to the street to find Ecstacy and Vicodin. That was part of his job. Mark convinced Paul to implement a budget strictly for Slim's drugs and liquor.Mark didn't know anybody in these foreign streets, but he copped Slim's drugs. He would make sure that Slim had the right Nikes to go with the right jeans. He would make sure Slim had new coats and gym shoes. He took care of Slim first and then took care of the rest of the crew. He made sure we all looked good. I really felt bad for Mark because I knew he wanted to whip Slim's ass. I told Mark, "Look, just because I am working for Slim and keeping myself between y'all doesn't mean I take his side." Honestly, Slim fucked up by putting his hands on Mark. He really fucked up. I told Mark that he should sue or ask for a hefty raise. Meanwhile, Slim was in the dressing room getting hyped. He was standing on the table giving his famous righthook speech, about how he knocks people out with his right hook. This speech only comes when he's drunk and high or he's either had a fight or he's ready to fight. Everybody was laughing at him. I chose to stand in the hallway, separate from Slim, because I didn't want to appear to be taking sides. I didn't see the fight; I just heard the altercation and intervened. Mark was trying his best to get back to Slim, and if he had succeeded, it would have been ugly.

Thinking back, the second trip to Stockholm, Sweden, was when Slim's personality started to unravel. Slim Shady crossed over into the persona of Marshall Mathers. He started to believe all the shit he rapped about; he started to believe his own hype. He started to believe that he could do or say anything to anybody. He was biting the hand that fed him. Mark took care of him even while at home. Mark would get him free clothes and have them sent to his house and my house. I think that was the shittiest thing Slim could have done. Things like that you just don't make up for no matter how many times you apologize. Mark let Slim know that shit every chance he got. Now that everyone was separated, Paul was sitting in the hallway worried that Slim was going to come at him to tell him to fire Mark. Mark was Paul's boy. Paul was confronted with a decision he didn't want to make. He realized he wasn't the big boss he pretended to be, rather he was no different from me—we both worked for Slim Shady. Paul tried to glorify his position many times, but in reality he worked for Slim just like the rest of us did. He always acted arrogant, like he was better than the rest of us. This was the first time I had seen him confused. He always thought he knew the right answers, but this time he didn't know what to do. He was in a dilemma. I just sat back and watched the whole thing unravel. I thought to myself, Slim is really losing it! He is losing it! It was only going to get worse. This was the first sign of Marshall Mathers losing his identity to Slim Shady.

After the fight, we sent Mark back to the hotel in a separate vehicle from Slim, and in the midst of everything, all of these young groupies were gathered out in front of the hotel. Kessia was with us, and we went in so Slim could sign some autographs. Kessia sat down, and who sat right by her? Agnes, the fifteen-year-old super-groupie! Agnes saw Kessia with Slim but tried to be friendly by providing Kessia with too much information. I don't know what the conversation was about. What I do know is that Kessia's mood totally changed from the time we were at the venue to the time we were in the hotel room. By this time, Slim had reached his peak of being drunk and high. He was being arrogant and loud and was really ego-tripping at this point. He wasn't caring about anyone's feelings or emotions. I told him, "You are playing it kind of close.You know, Agnes sat down right next to Kessia. They were talking and, to be honest, Kessia didn't look too happy." He was like,"Well, where is Kessia at?" I said, "She went back downstairs. She's not in the room right now." He was like, "Well, fuck it! Fuck it."

Really, Kessia was in the room next to ours, and both windows were open. Kessia was hanging out the window looking at the view. She looked depressed from the stress of the tour, and it was only the second day. Kessia was sitting there listening while Slim was bragging about what he did to Agnes in the bathroom, how he sexed her up, how he fingered her, and how she gave him some head.We reminded him that he was cutting it close with Kessia. His response was,"Man, I don't give a fuck about none of these bitches! Fuck these hos! I don't give a fuck about Kessia! I don't give a fuck about her! Shit! I do what the fuck I want to do!" I was like, "Damn! What's that all about?" Slim said he was tired of muthafuckas telling him what to do. "Man, ain't anybody trying to tell you nothing. I'm just saying, man, you are playing it a little bit close. I can only cover you for so many lies, man. Other than that, you're on your own!" After my brief conversation with Slim on trying to be a playboy, I went to the window to get some air, and who do I see? It's Kessia, crying. She looked at me with a smile to let me know that she was OK, but she had tears in her eyes. Immediately, I knew she heard everything that had been said. She was hurt, and I thought that was real fucked up. She was beyond being a groupie. She had proven herself to be a sweet girl. I didn't think anyone deserved to be treated like that. Slim had shitted on this young lady. She had overheard him, and there was no way he could deny it.We didn't say anything to each other; we each just closed our windows. I told Slim, "Guess what? While you were in here saying all those things, Kessia was right in the next room." He said,"How do you know?" And I said, "Because I saw her sitting right there in the window, and she had tears in her eyes, man. She heard everything you were saying." He was like, "For real?" and his whole mood changed, and he was like, "Well, I'll get with y'all later," and he went into his room to try to make things right. She never said anything to him about it. I know one thing; she gave him NO ASS that night! He only hit that one time throughout the whole tour because of that situation. He was mad. I said, "Man, you going to fly a mistress out, spend $7,000 on her, and treat her like that?"You should have at least been trying to get $7,000 worth of ass. This is your fault, man.You treated her like a third-class citizen.You spent all that money to get her out here, and your total focus should have been on her. You are sitting up here paying for steak, chewing on chicken nuggets, man. You got to be smarter." He always did dumb shit; that's what he chose to do.

It was October 27th, and we were flying from Stockholm to Berlin, and everybody was tripping that it was only the third day of the tour and all of this drama jumped off already, and the tour wasn't scheduled to end until the 17th of November. It seemed like we had been on tour a few weeks already, and everybody was like, "Man, we got a long way to go." I was thinking about my wife and kids, and I was looking at Slim in a different light and didn't like what I was seeing. Since I was working for him, I really wasn't at liberty to express my opinions; I was just making my money. We made it to Berlin and did a hype show, but what I remember most is how Slim and Paul treated this one VIP—they treated this guy like scum. Slim wanted to go to Niketown before his show. It was Paul, Slim, Patrice, this black guy in Berlin who is the host of the MTV video show over there, and me. Patrice and I got close on our first trip to Berlin, and he was a cool guy—he pretty much went out of his way to accommodate people. He did a lot to make us feel happy and comfortable in Germany. But every time he would ask a question just to be conversational, Slim and Paul would cut him down, saying things like, "Man, why the fuck would you ask a stupid question like that!" I was wondering why they were talking to him like that because he didn't deserve that. I mean, they were really getting beside themselves. They felt like they could talk to anybody any kind of way, but they failed to realize that someone was going to do them the same way one day because they were bullies. Paul tried to bully the whole crew like he was above the rest of us, but I always told him, "I work for Slim, I don't work for you." But Paul had this way of getting into Slim's head and controlling his brain like a puppet. He would tell Slim what to say, what to do, and how to react. It's a shame to see a grown man be influenced like that. Slim basically followed Paul's lead in talking down to Patrice the way they did. Later on, Patrice told me I was the nicest guy out of the bunch and related to me how he felt about Slim and Paul treating him like shit. I was like, "Man, I noticed that, but you need to speak up to them and not let them do that to you." He was like, "Man, I only have to deal with them once or twice a year, so I'm not even going to sweat it because I have business to conduct." I said, "Well, anything you need Slim to do don't ask Paul, ask me, and I can help you get it done. These guys go out of their way to be assholes, and it's not fair to you or a lot of other people that they do it to. The best thing for you to do is not take it personally." He agreed and told me again how nice a person I was.

That night, we experienced our first trip on a European tour bus. It was nothing to brag about. Picture this: a 6'8" black man, 320 pounds, in Europe. I'm like a giant over there because most of the people over there are skinny. If you see somebody fat over there the first thing you want to ask them is, "How did that happen?" When they say European cut, they mean that. That is no joke. European cut means "too small for your big ass." I found that out quickly. The tour bus was my second lesson in this situation. The tour bus I'm used to is about the size of a diesel truck with a trailer attached to it. The European tour bus was about half the size of that bus. It was sharp, but it was narrow and tight. Imagine ten people in half a tour bus. The beds were set up like coffins. I had to test each bed to see which one I could fit in. In one of them, the ceiling was so low I couldn't even get in—period. I finally found a bed I could fit in, but I had to maneuver my legs in first, hang out the bed, then push the rest of my body in in order to fit! It was such a tight fit that I couldn't sleep on my side because my shoulder would touch the top of the next bunk, and I couldn't sleep straight because my legs were too long. Ultimately, I had to be creative—I had to sleep with one leg hanging out of the bunk and the other leg folded up and, needless to say, that wasn't very comfortable at all. I wasn't looking forward to going through three weeks of that shit.

On top of that, the food was terrible. They didn't believe in regular food—all they served us was pork and rabbit food (vegetables) and you really couldn't get full. I must have lost about fifteen pounds on that tour. If you did eat any of the food over there, it tore up your stomach. We all must have had the runs for about a week. Another problem was that the bathroom on the bus was like five feet high and three feet wide, so that totally eliminated me from using the bathroom. When I went to the bathroom, I had to stand on the stairs that led to the bathroom, pee in a cup, and then pour the pee into the toilet. And forget about taking a dump because it wasn't even happening. My ass is three feet wide. I couldn't even get in the door—period, so it was torture. Between the food and the restroom facilities in Europe, by this time I was really missing home. And we had one cell phone on the bus, which was used to communicate with the US, like Interscope and home.

At night, we would take turns using the phone. I would always wait until nighttime when everyone else was asleep to call home, since Europe was six hours ahead anyway. I would rather wait than stand in line behind everyone else to call the US. The only bad part about that was if my wife or someone were to call, I would never get the message because so many people used the phone that we wouldn't get our messages for a couple of days, so I always made it a point to call home at least twice a day. Other than that, we still had the other problems, like the Mark and Slim situation. Mark was still pissed, and I couldn't blame him. He was going to quit, but Paul convinced him to stay on, and Slim was kissing his ass and was real apologetic whenever he was sober, which was usually a short-lived moment in the morning. That was basically the pattern on the tour. For about a week, the Mark and Slim situation was the hot topic. Kessia wasn't opening up to Slim, figuratively and literally, and she spoke to me about overhearing the things Slim said about her, so of course she was hurt. She was ready to go home, but all she did was smoke some weed to pacify her feelings and try to make Slim miserable in the process, and that's what he deserved.

On October 29th, we were in Chemnitz, Germany, the ghetto of all ghettos.This ghetto was worse than any ghetto you can imagine in the US. On top of that, this was an area in Germany where there used to be Nazi concentration camps. That made Mark Labelle nervous because he was a Jew. I wasn't really nervous because I had dealt with the Nazis before, as well as the Klan, so I had nothing to worry about. But Mark was as nervous as a dog in a Chinese restaurant.We all stuck together, and no one went out of his or her way to do anything extra because it was really dark there. I mean dark all the time. It was depressing! You could actually sense the racial problems they had in the past. It was sick, seeing all the racial slurs written on the walls, seeing the bunkers and the locked-up sheds with racial graffiti on them. It was sick. It looked exactly like the concentration camps we had seen in our history books.We couldn't wait to get the fuck out of there. It was eerie.We did a hype show, but I told Slim I had a bad feeling about the place and warned him not to do any stage dives that night. I told him, "As the Nazis tell it, they can't stand any of us, so don't jump off the stage tonight because you could get stabbed or something." They weren't known for shootings, but they were known for stabbings in that particular part of Germany. Fortunately, he listened to me, and we did the show and we got the hell out of there.

A few days had gone by, and we did a few more shows, and everyone was trying to get accustomed to this small tour bus with its limited amount of sitting and standing space. It was horrible. Slim was getting tired of Kessia being on the tour, and he was going to cut her little vacation short. All she wanted to do was see Amsterdam, but she was supposed to be on for the length of the entire tour. Kessia and Slim were getting tired of each other, and she wasn't giving him any sex. He was hurting, so he started making preparations to fly in another young lady, Nicole, from California, whom he had met during the Hawaii Death Row incident. He started making up this story to tell Kessia, that he was flying his "girl" out. He always referred to Kim as his girl and not his wife. Kessia knew about Kim, but Kim didn't know about Kessia. He proceeded to tell Kessia this story that he and Kim were having some problems, and that he needed to see her in order to work them out. This was just to get Kessia out of there, since she wasn't giving him any sex. I really couldn't blame her. He wasn't treating her right, so she cut off the goods. She was like,"Well, I guess I'm not going to make it to Amsterdam, huh?" Slim said, "No. I'm going to send you home on November 2nd." She was upset about that. I told her to just look at this like it was a little vacation. "Now you can go home and tend to whatever personal business you may have." At least, now you see how he operates. This is his lifestyle. He is going to run through a lot of people like toilet paper. He's going wipe himself then throws them away.

I told her it was unfortunate that she had to go through this but to take it as a lesson.We all would go through it in some way. She thanked me for the advice and said I always managed to say the right things. I told her how I really didn't want to come back out on this tour. I would have rather stayed home and resolved some of my own family issues and spent more time with my sons and made things right with my wife. She told me that Slim told her that about me, but that he needed me with him because I was like a positive force for him, and he knew that things would get done with me being there. My total focus was always on him. I wasn't chasing any women or smoking any weed. I wasn't taking any Ecstasy or Vicodin. Sometimes Slim and Paul would ask me to take something with them. I would decline every time. I always felt as if they were testing me. If I had, then they would have something to hold against me. I always told them, "I'm not here for that. If I were to do that, then who would take care of y'all?" I was trying to do the right thing. It felt good to hear Kessia tell me Slim felt that I was a positive influence. I feel that he meant it, but unfortunately, Paul has that man's mind in the palm of his hands. Slim never did express how he really felt. The sad part of it all is that Slim's not going to realize this until it's too late, when Paul is finished using him and throws him away. Slim's going to find himself alone. Everyone around him sees this, but he either can't see it or he won't see it.

Between Mark's black eye, Kessia being disrespected, and Slim's sexual escapades with minors, things were unbearable. I felt as if there was not one positive thing coming out of this whole tour. I knew I had to find something to keep my mind focused and to keep myself from being depressed, because everybody was depressed on this tour. People were depressed about their money not being right while these groupies were being flown out, and things of that nature. People weren't feeling

Slim's crew celebrating Platinum success in the UK.

as though they were being treated fairly, and it was only the first week of the tour. A lot of tension had been carried over from previous tours, and it was building up. You could hear people saying that this would be their last tour and things like that. I even promised myself that this would be my last European tour, and my only recourse to keep my sanity was to get deeper and deeper into my Bible. That's all I had. I had the Lord, I had my faith, I had the thoughts of my wife and kids, I had their pictures that I kept inside my Bible that I kissed good night every night, and that's all I had to keep me going. I got into my Bible like never before, because among so many negative elements, that's all I had to look to. I couldn't run from it because I was there. This European tour let me reinvent myself. It let me look back on my mistakes of the past, and try to correct things and handle things the right way. I was looking at Slim and seeing the mistakes that he was making and I was like, Man, this guy is going to have hell to pay. I mean, I know people can change their ways, but he was doing one negative thing after another.

It was November 2nd, and we were in Stuttgart, Germany, and this was to be Kessia's last day on the tour. She was ready to go home after the nonsense she had been going through, accompanied by the embarrassment and the way Slim was talking to her. He would make comments in front of everyone like, "Kessia, when you going to give me some head, when you going to give me some pussy?" He would be saying it jokingly, but you could tell he really meant that shit.That's the way he used to play; he would say shit in a joking manner, but you could tell he was dead serious. He belittled her, and she had finally reached a point where she realized she didn't have to deal with that shit. She had taken all she could take, and from talking to her, I could tell she was ready to go. She had also figured out that he was flying in someone else, and it wasn't his wife.What Slim saw in Kessia was that she was someone he could communicate with. They could laugh together, plus she was a nice-looking young lady. I guess he started letting the fame go to his head. He decided he needed bigger and better things, he needed finer women. He needed more. At one time, Kessia was his whole world. I remember when we were leaving Phoenix, Arizona, and he told Kessia he loved her on the cell phone. However, he was high on Ecstasy. From what I understand, Ecstasy can do those things to you. She was his way to escape. He didn't deal with all the drama with Kessia that he did with Kim, his wife.

On November 3rd, we reached Zurich, Switzerland. For some reason, at this one show, a local group strong-armed the promoter to let them perform at this venue.We found out about this after all the drama happened. We had the largest dressing room, but the dressing room was like Grand Central Station because each group had to pass through our dressing room to get to the stage. This is where the drama started. The group that strong-armed the promoter was comprised of some Haitians, and everywhere we went, to do interviews, for example, they tried to come through, but I always shut them down. I told them, "Man, back up.We are doing an interview, so back up," and they would pretend they couldn't speak English, but I had heard them speak English earlier. I said, "Man don't play, just get back, and speak English when you talk to me." They said, "Well, we're just trying to get back to our dressing room," and I was like, "Well, whatever. Y'all just have to wait because we are in here conducting interviews, so y'all can't be running through here with your people and your little groupies or whatever." So, the promoter stepped in and was like, "Well, they need to get to their dressing rooms," and I was like, "Well, y'all should have given us a different dressing room because we don't want all this traffic running through here.We got valuable stuff in here, and if people come in here and take our stuff there's gonna be a problem."

So the promoter talked to these guys and told them to notify us before going into our dressing room. They ignored that, though, because when we were onstage they were all in our dressing room, eating Slim's food and drinking Slim's liquor and the whole nine. There was no one who could stop them since our room was on the way to their room. Upon our return to our room, we found that we had basically been looted. Luckily, however, we hid the "Chronic 2001" tape, because it could have been stolen and bootlegged. I always felt like Slim's road manager/babysitter. I always had to make sure he kept up with the "Chronic 2001" tape before the release. I often found myself carrying his tapes and his rhyme books around, plus keeping up with his personal property. I can recall a time in California when Slim thought he lost his rhyme book. I had to look every place we had been in the last twenty-four hours, only to find out that he left it at the studio. Those types of situations always made me feel like I wasn't being paid enough.With this situation, with this group stealing our liquor, Mark and I basically had to go fetch it from these guys' dressing room. Of course, this group fronted and was speaking shit in a foreign language. They were too scared to speak in English because they knew they would get their asses kicked. We took back the little bit of liquor that was left for Slim.

After a show, Slim's crew liked to smoke their weed and get drunk. Slim was angry about our liquor being boosted.We told the promoter of the show what happened. I knew this group was going to be trouble from the beginning.We wanted them out of our area—period! We ended up throwing them out of their dressing room. Their little female manager came to say something about us "sharing." She tried to be cute, but we weren't going for it. "The group had already strong-armed their way on to the show, then stole our liquor. Please! We have no words for y'all. Ain't nobody coming back through here—NOBODY!" She was mad, speaking that German shit again. Regardless, we put them out. So our crew started to cool out and the promoter bought us some more liquor. Then one of the Haitian guys from the local group decided to come up and battle Slim in a battle rap. He was outside our door talking to Proof, who didn't know these guys had tried to give us a problem earlier because he wasn't around, so he brought him into our dressing room. I was like, "Yo, what is my man doing in here?" They were exchanging numbers. I said, "Y'all are going to have to do that outside! They were stealing our shit earlier." The guy from the local group was like, "Anyway!" I cut him off. "Anyway nothing! You come up in here keeping up traffic, starting all that shit earlier, stealing our shit and now you want to come and politic with us? Fuck that shit! You got to get the fuck out!" Proof didn't know all that shit went down. The guy still had his pen in his hand from trying to get Proof's number.The dude gave me a funny look. I grabbed his wrist because I didn't know if he was going to try to stab Proof or me with the pen. Then he was reaching for his pocket, so I grabbed that arm. I shook him up, then threw him out of our room. He tried to say some words. I told him, "If you come back in here, I will beat the shit out of you, flat out! Just because we are in your country, don't think you won't get your ass whipped!"

The promoter then came into our room to see what the problem was. I said, "It's those same guys you let on the show—that weren't even supposed to be on the show—keeping up all kinds of shit. I want them out of this building." Now, the venue had a hotel attached to it, and the guys were staying at the hotel and kept sending people down to start shit, so I told that group, "If y'all are going to do something, do it, because I'm not going to keep going back and forth with y'all. Nobody has time for this shit!" Now, when I thought of Switzerland, I thought of snow and ski slopes, pretty women, furs, and diamonds. The last thing I expected was to be getting into it with some ghetto people at a show. We ended up getting out of there without anything happening, but these guys were some unruly characters. Finally, we signed a few autographs, got on the bus, and we were out!

November 4th, 1999 – Offenbach, Germany

Nicole, the one from LA, had arrived. She was fine, too; she was definitely hot. She made all the women Slim has ever dealt with look like beauty pageant trainees. She was gorgeous. She was Puerto Rican and Mexican mixed. When I first met her, I didn't care too much for her, but she turned out to be good people. She was wealthy and really didn't seem to want for anything. She seemed to have more than Slim, to be honest with you. My first impression of her was that she thought her shit didn't stink, that she was arrogant and snooty, but all in all, she was nice. Plus, Europe has a way of making people adjust. Besides, you can't have two arrogant, obnoxious people in the same room—that would be her and Slim. She was the only female who kept Slim in check. She didn't play those little word games when he would ask her for head in front of everyone. Sister didn't play that. She was cool. She read a lot, and we got close. For some strange reason, all of Slim's mistresses would confide in me. I guess because, aside from Proof and myself, we were the most levelheaded people there. We were always sober and driven by family. She was family oriented too, because she had a little girl. She knew who to talk to and who was full of shit. She also brought a different feel to the tour. By the time she arrived things were looking better because we were all adjusting to being over there.

Our stomachs were feeling better as we adapted. We even found a Kentucky Fried Chicken to make up for all the pork we had been served. Things were looking better, but of course Slim had spent $4,000 to fly Nicole to Europe. At this point, none of that even mattered because we knew where we stood. We knew, his crew and me, his bodyguard, that we weren't his first priority. Therefore, we lacked in loyalty as he lacked in appreciation for us. That's basically where we stood.

We boarded the tour bus on November 5th, heading for Koln. Koln was the spot. It was everything we thought it would be. Koln was the best part of the tour for many of us. It reminded me of Manhattan mixed with Paris. There were a lot of English-speaking people there and a wide variety of ethnic groups, as well, from Indians to Germans to Ethiopians to Italians. A lot of military guys were there, too. Probably some of the most beautiful women in the world stayed in Koln. I mean, they were hot! Stockholm had some fine women, but Koln had some exotic women. The women looked like Vanity, Apollonia, Jennifer Lopez—they were built and always wore spandex and halter tops—it was a nice sight to see. And they loved American men, especially black men. To be from Detroit was the icing on the cake. Slim rocked the show, and it was off the chain. All the shows were basically the same – same show, different city. The fun started after the show. I figured Slim was in with Nicole, so it was my chance to get out and see some sights.

I had basically been cooped up for the entire road trip, catering to Slim and running him around. Koln was a nice city with a lot of nice restaurants, nice American restaurants. At this point, I had lost about ten pounds, so I felt like I had a lot of catching up to do. And I was looking to get out and see some sights. When I had some downtime, Proof was my hanging partner. On this particular night, we got together with some people we had met. One guy owned a clothing store with his cousin and sister. They were Ethiopians and were pretty cool. They took us out to what they considered their hood, but again, there were all different races and all these exotic-looking women. We went to one bar, and the setup was that you would pay and get a ticket, and when you got something from the bar, you got your ticket punched and paid for all your punches as you were leaving the club. You had to keep good track, because at the end they would hit you up. Upon entering the club, everyone had to have a double shot of Absolute and cranberry juice. I thought it was cool that they set you up like that at the beginning. The five of us went in, and they were playing nothing but American music, everything from Puffy to Jay-Z to 95 South, and I mean the DJ was on jam. I felt like I was back at home. Proof and I were just relaxing, having some drinks and getting a lot of attention because we didn't really fit in; we weren't dressed like everybody else and looked like we were from the States.Women were coming around us, hoping we would talk to them, but Proof and I were waiting for the music to come on that we wanted to dance to, and then we were going to ask some ladies to dance.

The people we were with were already dancing and were asking us when we were going to dance, and I was like, "Hold on. I'll be out there to show you a little something."We were having a ball. It was hot as hell in that club, and I had on a T-shirt and flannel. Needless to say, it didn't take long at all before I came out of that flannel. The DJ started really bumping, so I grabbed this one young lady, and I guess folks didn't think a man of my 6'8", 320 pound stature could put it down like I did. I have always been a good dancer, and I don't think there's a man out there my size who can dance as well as I can. I was showing her how we do it in Detroit, and I was breaking it down from the old to the new, and I knew I was throwing down because the floor had cleared up and all the women were staring in awe. Next thing I knew, Proof grabbed a girl and was doing his thing, and Proof and I turned the club out.We danced with these girls for at least forty-five minutes, and there were ladies waiting in line to dance with us.

Every time we would come off the floor, someone else would come up right away and ask us to dance. Then we saw people trying to imitate our dance moves, and that, for me, was the most fun part of the tour. I really enjoyed myself. It gave me a chance to forget about Slim.When he goes to a club, you can forget about having any fun at all. You always have to watch for him to get into a fight or for someone to bump him, and the man has a bladder the size of a peanut. Every five minutes, he would have to go to the bathroom, which meant that I would have to follow him to the bathroom. He drank like a fish, and as quickly as the liquor went in, it came out. If he wanted to holler at a girl, I would have to hang nearby to let him do his thing and not crowd his space. If we were in a place where there were a lot of guys who knew who he was but were giving him grim looks, I would stick close by him. I never let anyone get close to him or do anything to him. But Koln was a nice time, a real good time.

The only thing that sticks in the back of my mind about Koln that made me feel like I was some kind of a robot was when Slim and Nicole wanted to go shopping. I was like, "OK, give me a few minutes because I have to use the bathroom." Number two that is. So I'm doing my thing and not five minutes later Slim is banging on the door trying to rush me, threatening to leave without me. I was like, "So be it if that's what you choose to do. Damn, can I take a shit?" I mean, I wasn't going to have a sequel to it later on. I said, "I am allowed to take one shit a day, right? Just give me a moment in here!" He still was trying to rush me, and I was like, "Man, I am not rushing this. This is my personal time," blah, blah, blah. "If y'all are in that much of a rush, then go! I don't appreciate you rushing me when I'm letting nature take its course." Finally, he went and waited in the lobby. To me, he was trying to play big shot in front of Nicole to give the image that he doesn't even allow his people to take a shit, and when he says, "Let's go," it is time to go, but that wasn't the case on that day because I was taking my time. That shit pissed me off, and I told him how I felt. I said, "Are you in that much of a rush where I can't even take a shit? The stores don't close for another six hours. C'mon man, its not that serious." He tried to laugh it off, and Nicole was looking at me like, "Damn, a man's got to do what a man's got to do, you know?" That was the only negative memory I have of Koln.

A few days passed, and thank God we were on our way out of Germany into the UK to do some shows. The shows went well. Nothing spectacular happened except that on the 9th, Slim had a gold party for the UK sales. I got a chance to take some pictures of him with a couple of the Spice Girls. I now understand why they call that girl Scary Spice. Her acne was so fucking bad, it looked like someone was playing connect-the-dots on her face, plus she had a real shitty attitude. She was not nice at all. Regardless, the gold party went well, and we were all supposed to be presented plaques for the success of the Slim Shady Tour, but unfortunately the person who was responsible for the plaques lost all of them—how I do not know. On November 10th, we had made it to Glasgow, Scotland. That place was pretty cool. Slim slept in there, so I had a chance to go out and do some shopping for my family, as well as do some sightseeing. I bought my wife a real nice crystal glass slipper for the curio cabinet. For me, that was a symbol that I would do anything for her, because when I was in Europe I realized that I needed to grow and to reinvent myself. I had been fasting for the past six days because I knew we were going to Amsterdam and that was the place where I made a mistake on the last tour, drinking the mushroom tea, eating the hash brownies—I was totally out of character. I was trying to blend in and have some fun during my downtime, but all I did was demonstrate stupidity to the highest level.

This time, I was going to be prepared because Amsterdam was no joke. It is a place where you can basically do whatever you want to do. If you want to smoke weed, then you can smoke weed; if you want to piss outside, they have these little holes where you can piss outside; if you want to go get a prostitute, they have an area where you can do that, and the prostitutes are actually pretty nice looking. For me, being married and everything, I was fasting to cleanse my soul and strengthen my discipline. I mean, you see a lot of guys doing their thing over there, but for me that would get to my conscience. I was preparing myself to go home because the end of the tour was approaching, as well, and a lot of us were tired at this point. Glasgow was going to be Nicole's last spot. Slim was going to be doing a lot of photo shoots for his album there, and he wasn't going to have much time for her so he went ahead and sent her back. One thing we found out about the women in Scotland was that they don't drink beer, they drink bourbon, scotch—hard liquor—and they drink it straight. And they can out drink any man in the US!

We were off on the 11th to Amsterdam, and I was taking some time out to do some reflection and preparing myself to go home on the 13th. I was also preparing myself for my resignation as Slim's bodyguard. I felt as though I had seen enough; I mean, what else could there be? I felt like, from my experiences and from my reading, especially my reading of the Bible, that I had seen everything that I needed to see. I had been all around the world damn near twice, and I felt like I had gathered all the necessary resources for me to get my own label together and get my own group, the Wadsquad, off the ground. By this time, Slim and Paul had made it clear that they weren't going to be increasing my pay. I weighed this all against the fact that I was missing the constant growth of my baby boy. My eldest son was getting smarter and smarter. The responsibility on my wife's shoulders was getting to be overwhelming. This had to come to an end.

The idea came to me at this time to write this book. I still had my job with General Motors to go back to. The primary reason for my fasting was so that the Lord would give me clarity about my decisions. All I wanted was a clean break from Slim and Paul. I wasn't going to do anything to jeopardize my pay, I was going to work as they needed me to until the tour ended in December and just resign in January. I felt as though I could gain no more. I took this whole experience working with him as an internship, a lesson that brought me even closer to God. I learned to lean on the Lord more than to depend on man. Depending on Paul and Slim was a letdown every time.They were extremely undependable.They had no idea that a man's word is his bond. They were so quick to make a promise and then renege. I was raised that your word is your bond—it is all you have, and without that, you have nothing. Plus, I knew that I was worth more than what they were paying. I was worth more than they thought I was.

This period made me look back over history at slavery and servitude. I knew I was no servant, but I was definitely making slave wages. I never wanted to bring up racial issues, but I have to say that Slim and Paul were very smooth in masquerading their attitudes toward the blacks in the Shady camp. The way they showed their racial attitudes was in the way they paid people. How are you going to pay a sound man $1,500 for two and a half hours of work, five days a week, but yet you pay the security guy who works 24-7 – meaning if you go to the bathroom or want to go see a girl in the middle of the night he has to be there – only $1,200 a week?? I was on call twenty-four hours, and my workdays consisted of seventeen hours. I got a minimal amount of sleep. At that point, I realized that I couldn't be their house nigger any longer; I couldn't be their token anymore – it wasn't going to happen. I got everything together as far as my music, my resources, and my connections.

I had met a lot of important people during this tour. When Slim would do his interviews, my job was to coordinate who would see him next, and I would slide these people my business card. I would politic with them briefly, exchange information, and stay in touch with them when I got home. I realized, through reading my Bible and being away from home, that I belonged back at home raising my own family and not away raising this man while he was raising hell. It took that trip to Europe, which I didn't want to go on, to realize this. When you are that far away from your family on the other side of the world, it doesn't matter how much money you are making. I realized the truth in the adage that money cannot buy happiness. Slim is a prime example of this because the man has a lot of money, but he is miserable—the man is miserable! His wife doesn't make him happy; the music doesn't make him happy; only his daughter makes him happy. He hates to be alone, and he can't sleep alone without taking something like a Vicodin to help him sleep. He is not happy. He chases his breakfast of cheese eggs with Ecstasy. He would take one half, then the other half a couple of hours later. It was routine, and I got tired of that.

What was the point of me watching this man destroy his life? If I have to sit back and watch some man destroy himself, at least let me get paid right for it. At least let me get paid right if I have to watch this man throw his life down the tubes. He and I had a conversation once where he told me that he felt like he didn't need the drugs to do a show anymore, whereas once upon a time he felt dependent on them. I told him to stop, but apparently he didn't have the discipline necessary to do so at that time. He asked me how I remained so disciplined all the time, and I told him it was God. I can recall the one time I saw him read a Bible, and that was because I presented it to him. That was after a big blowout argument he had with Kim on the phone toward the end of the tour, at a point after he sent Nicole home. He wanted to fly Kim out for the rest of the tour, as he was feeling guilty about flying the other two girls out. He had the feeling that Kim was cheating on him because he had set her up in an apartment, and she was never there, no matter what time he called. So, all of a sudden he wanted to play the family man. I can't blame him for that either, nor do I blame him for any of the things he did on the road because I am sure Kim was doing her share of dirt, as well.

I can remember one day Slim and Kim got into a big argument, and I had never seen him so upset. He was red and teary eyed but he didn't cry. He was frustrated. On the day when he advised Nicole she would be going home, it was no big deal to her because she always had nice things, and she always traveled, so she was cool with it. However, Slim was in this lounge looking absolutely miserable. He looked devastated that he had all this money but was still miserable because of the way he was brought up. He's not a cultured man. A lot of times I tried to cultivate and support him, even when I knew he was wrong, because I felt like anybody could be changed at any given moment to do better. I was his biggest supporter. I'm not one to judge. So what I did at that moment was the only thing I could do. I gave him my Bible and told him to read Psalm 121. I said, "Slim, meet God; God, meet Slim. You should read this every day, man. I'm not trying to force religion on you, but this is how I make it through all this nonsense in the world and in this industry." I always told Slim not to let this industry pull him away from his family, where his family was second. I had started to follow my own advice because I saw how the game had taken me away and changed me. Luckily, I was able to get back to work and myself as a better, new and improved Byron Williams; a better, new and improved husband; a better, new and improved father; a better, new and improved businessman. I had gained so much on this tour but at the same time lost so much in the making. I gave Slim that Bible, and he read it, and he came out and said, "Thanks, Naz," and hugged me. I felt good knowing that I had done something positive for this man and, for that moment, changed him in some way. I knew it was going to take more than one time, but I felt good presenting him that material to read at that time, and that is the way I tried to support him from time to time.

November 12th – the dreaded Amsterdam

The one thing I didn't have to worry about was making the same mistake twice. This go-round to Amsterdam was pretty mild. I am glad I did what I did the last time I was there, though, to get it out of my system, but what's done is done. Well, everyone was feeling sick again, and we were also tired and recuperating from the little tour bus and happy to be going home soon. The tour was scheduled to end on the 17th, and Slim was ready to go home and deal with his family problems, and everyone was ready to go home. The tour was short in actual time, but a lot of long events happened. The show was real hype that night. From what I understand, the Amsterdam crowd doesn't get hype for a lot of people because they are all too high to do so, but they got up for Slim. It was probably one of the most hype shows given there. Proof basically took the show because he jumped up from the stage to the balcony. I don't know how he did it. He was sliding down poles and everything. The only incident we had was when this guy was trying to grab Slim's leg and pull him off the stage, but I snatched the guy out of the crowd and threw him down some stairs backstage. MTV had it all on tape.We were supposed to leave the day after the show, but everything was thrown off schedule because instead we flew to the MTV Music Awards. That went smoothly, and we decided to end the tour early on the 14th and lie to the people, telling them that Slim took ill and was unable to finish the tour.

The rest of the tour was scheduled to take place in Germany, and none of us were looking forward to going back to Germany. Germany had some good people there, but it was overall a depressing place. So we were in Amsterdam to do the photo shoot, and Slim decided that he didn't want to do it, just like in New York. A $10,000 photo shoot, and we're going through this again. Mark was trying to get Slim up, and Slim didn't want to get out of bed. Mark called Paul, who was not in any big rush to come out of his room to help get Slim out of bed. So, Mark asked me to see if I could talk to Slim to get him out of bed. I was like, "Man, why do y'all always come to me? This is not what I get paid to do." It seemed like I was the only one who could get through to him. I went into Slim's room about a half hour after Mark left and said, "All right, Slim, we got to go do this photo shoot." I turned on the shower, opened the curtains, and put the "Chronic 2001" tape in the box. I said, "C'mon man, tomorrow we get to go home and see our ladies and our children, and you know Hailey's going to be so happy to see you. C'mon, and let's get this day started."

It was 2:00 p.m. already, and we were supposed to do the shoot earlier that morning, but he wasn't going to do it at all. I told him, "If you don't do it now, they're just going to make you come back and do it on your off time, which costs more money. And if you want to quit your job, that's cool—you can always go back and work at Gilbert's." Finally, he got up and got into the shower, and I walked out. I guess the mention of Gilbert's hit a sore spot. Gilbert's is where he used to wash dishes before he got his deal, but they fired him a few years back on Christmas. The mention of that place always worked on Slim.Anyway,Amsterdam was full of a lot of important record executives, who were Paul's buddies. Paul's friends were cool—they acted nothing like Paul. Paul was an asshole. Anyway, there was Shecky Green, the president of Game Records; Stretch Armstrong from Hot 97; Reef, one of the top producers—all of the bigwigs were there, and we didn't know why, but we knew it was something important. Anytime you see those guys, it's definitely about business. There's some money involved in the music industry. Me and Proof kicked it around to see if we could find out what they were doing there, but they kept it on the down low. They could have been just vacationing or something, because they definitely had money like that to kick it. Regardless, Amsterdam went smoothly, Slim did his photo shoot, and the next day we were supposed to go home.

I was looking forward to that because it was the beginning of the new me—the first day of the rest of my life.We told Mike (the European tour manager) to hook us up with a straight flight from Amsterdam to Detroit, no connectors or any of that shit, and he did. Everything worked out pretty good, and we went home.

6

HOME SWEET HOME

On November 14th, we touched down in Detroit. It felt good to beback, and it felt good to have a new outlook on life; it felt good to have done some soul searching and to have reinvented myself. I found out what Byron Williams was all about because I knew what everyone else was all about. Now, I really know who I am. Sometimes a little solitary confinement is good, and that's what being in Europe meant to me.Terrible food, being away from my family, isolation and minimal money–to me that was solitary confinement. I had a lot of time to think, and this was the most influential time for my family and me because I felt purged.

I got the family together, and we went on our yearly trip up north to a hotel room and ate breakfast and let the kids play. It was a special time for me because I was able to make up for lost time and bond with my family, especially my baby boy, because he and I never had a chance to do so since I was always on the road. This time, I had a nice little break, and I knew I probably wouldn't have to work again until the weekend, when Slim would probably want to go out, which wouldn't be a problem. I really enjoyed my time with my family, and I felt different. I felt revived. I felt as though I had seen all I needed to see, and it was time for me to be at home. Being in Europe on that bus, I had a lot of time to do some thinking. Referring to my Bible during my downtime really enabled me to put my life into perspective.One verse in particular that I came across really helped me to focus. It answered all of my questions. The verse was Proverbs 24,Verse 27. It said, "Prepare your outside work. Make it fit for yourself in the field and afterward build your house." I read that, and I said, "Man, that's hitting it right on the nose." I interpreted that as I had met all the people I needed to meet in this music business, and I had gone as high as possible working with Slim and meeting all the people that I met. I gathered all my resources and contacts and made them fit for myself, and it was time for me to go back home and build my family back up and get everything back together and make myself better. That verse sticks with me, and I'm sure I'm going to remember that for the rest of my life.

I was getting back into the swing of things at home, knowing at any time that could be interrupted by a call from Slim. I would call him at noon every day to see if he needed anything, but oftentimes I couldn't even speak to him. I would leave a message with his wife for him to call me on my cell. I was going to be out and about with my family. When he was at home, he felt like he didn't need me. I beg to differ, though, because I can recall one night after he had a big physical blowout with Kim, he went out walking to get some air alone in the hood of Detroit, away from where he and Kim usually stayed in the suburbs. He was walking by these two black guys at a pay phone who had a dog with them. One of them said, "What's up, man? You Slim Shady?" And he was like, "Yeah," and kept walking. The other guy called out, "Like, you Slim Shady for real?" and Slim was like, "Yeah," and turned around to give him a play, but the guy knocked him down and stomped him and kept hitting him. Eventually, he broke away and ran home, with his eye looking pretty bad. I told him he was lucky they didn't kill him and that he couldn't keep walking around like he wasn't famous.

"You're famous now, and there are jealous people out here who want to do something to you. Everybody doesn't want to be your friend or get your autograph. You have to be wiser than that. You have to be smarter. People see all these lawsuits in the paper, and they think you got major loot. That's why that happened." He then went back to the house to get Kim, and they did this Bonnie-and-Clyde thing, trying to ride down on the guys to get revenge. You would think one ass whipping would have been enough, but they were going back for more, like a combo deal. What he should have done was filed a police report, or at least called me. But instead, he put it upon himself to prove he's hard and go look for this guy, to look for more trouble.

Needless to say, he didn't find the guys, and he had to chalk it up as an ass whipping like he did. He called and told me everything the next day, and I was furious. I was like, "I know you were mad, but you can't go walking at that time of night thinking that people won't bother you, because people know who you are, man; they are going to notice you." The whole point was he felt like he could come home and do the same things he had been doing before he sold a couple of million records, but I told him, "Those days are over. You can't do that shit anymore. You can forget it. You're not a normal person anymore." All he wanted to do was be able to turn it on and turn it off, but I told him it didn't work like that.

I can recall one time when he took his daughter to a park way out in the suburbs, and she cut herself playing. While he was tending to her wounds, a groupie came up and asked him for his autograph, and he told the guy to get the fuck away. I thought that was the most inconsiderate thing a groupie could do. People just don't care. These fans think you owe them something for that $14.99 they pay for your CD and will go to any extent to get a piece of you. Anyway, the weekend of November 20th, he wanted to go hang out and show his face at some local clubs like the Shelter and St. Andrews Hall. He wanted people to know that he still came back to his roots. I tried to get him to do that often, but he didn't like to do it unless he was with his group, D-12. Anyway, this weekend when he called me and let me know that he, Kim, and D-12 wanted to go out. I took it upon myself to pick them up because I knew that they were going to get shit-faced drunk, and I would rather drive them than have them out drunk driving. Kim already had one DUI. Kim had a nice apartment in Sterling Heights that Slim signed for, even though he said he wasn't going to do that. There were seven people staying in a two-bedroom apartment, and I couldn't understand that for the life of me since Slim was sitting on millions. I guess he always lived like that so he was used to it, but personally, I couldn't do it. When I got to the apartment to pick them up, Kim's sister answered the door. She had this big-ass black eye and her eyeball was red. As I was talking to her, my eye started hurting just looking at it. She told me that she and Kim got into a fight, and Kim did that to her. I was thinking, "Damn, that's one hell of a punch!"

Kim's sister introduced me to her husband, and the first thing he did was deny giving her the black eye, and I was like, "Yeah, she just told me Kim did it." I was thinking, Damn, this is a mixture of "The Beverly Hillbillies" and "South Park." As I was sitting there on the couch, there were a couple of kids running around, being kids, and there were three cats there, causing my allergies to act up. I looked at the situation and realized that Slim was the only one working. There was Kim, his sister-in-law, and his brother-in-law and their children, and I was thinking, why? He moved from sleeping in a bunk bed at his mother-in-law's house into a convalescent home-type situation. I couldn't understand it. But that's the way he chose to live, with everybody there mooching off him. He was paying all the bills and buying all the food, and he complained about it but didn't do anything to change it. I told him to do something about it, to put their asses out or have them get a job or something, but don't sit there and complain about it and not do anything about it. But that's just how he chose to live.

We went out that night, and Kim was looking nice. She's an attractive woman, tall and a natural blond. She's very nice looking, but she has the shittiest attitude. This night, she was dressed nice and was showing off her new boobs that Slim paid for.They had cost him about five grand, and Slim and Paul got into a dispute about that. Lo and behold, Kim got her new tits, so I guess everybody was happy. I guess I would have done the same thing for her. They looked pretty nice on her. She was showing off her tits, and Slim didn't seem to mind, and we then headed out. Slim tried to drive, but I convinced him that it would be best for me to drive since they would be drinking. They wanted to go get some drinks, so we headed to Ruby Tuesday, and Slim got his Bacardi and Kim got a Hennessy. People noticed him, but no one really stepped over to him or anything; they would just walk by and wave.They tried to get me to drink and loosen up with them, but I refused, telling them that I had to be sober in case something jumped off.We all talked, and I actually had a good time. Kim even seemed to be in a good mood for a change.

We didn't have a problem with her that night, and I was shocked. We talked about how good it felt to be home and to go Christmas shopping, and I tried to set Slim up to go up north to the spot my family and I usually go, but their daughter was in the hospital with the flu. The trip, for them, was canceled. Anyway, we finished our drinks and headed to St. Andrews. Kim was showing me her new Rolex that Slim just bought her— it was all iced out with diamonds and was real nice. I mean, you are supposed to do that type of stuff for your lady, but I was calculating all the money that was being spent right before my eyes. I couldn't even get a raise.The watch had to have run at least ten grand, and I saw seven grand spent on Kessia coming out to Europe and another four grand on Nicole to Switzerland.That's twenty-one grand! No doubt, he was the boss, but at least take care of your people so that they feel appreciated. That's all people want–to feel appreciated. Finally, we left and headed to the club. On the way to the club we played the "Chronic 2001" tape and

Slim is trying to impress Kessia with the $7,000 he spent on her plane ticket to Berlin, Germany.

the song "What's the Difference" came on. Slim's verse was saying how he would kill Kim and drive around with her dead body, waving at people, and drop her off at the bus stop and toot the horn as he drives away, and I had to turn down the volume. I told them I wasn't sure how they felt but that that was awkward for me. Kim was like, "Yeah, isn't that some fucked up shit?" and Slim said, "It's only entertainment." It almost started an argument, but luckily it ceased.

Once we were at the club, I gave him his space because he was known there, and D-12 was there also, so I wasn't playing him too close. Other than some folks coming up kicking freestyles and passing demos, everything was cool, and my job wasn't hard that night. Slim and Kim had some nice buzzes going, and they wanted to leave and go shoot some pool at a place near the house. I called my people, the Wadsquad, and they came to shoot some pool, too, and the night went pretty smoothly. On the way home, Slim had to make his routine Taco Bell stop, then we went home. It turned out to be a good evening.

November 26th was Slim's homecoming show at the Royal Oak Music Theatre, featuring his group, D-12, Royce Da 5'9", and my own group, the Wadsquad, was opening up. I had basically politicked this show months earlier, but my group got played because our name wasn't even on the flyer, thanks to Paul. He claimed that he switched printers and that the information got lost in the transfer. I was like, "Whatever, man. We are going to rock it, anyway." I made sure that I told my crew to shit on everybody on the show, because they all had deals except us. I told my crew we had to be the best. When we left, everyone there knew who we were. We had the crowd super hyped. We had been rehearsing all week for it, and we stole the show. I got them a limo so they could feel what it was like to roll in celebrity fashion. We also did interviews with The Source and a radio station, and it was tight – it was a real good feeling. I felt like that was the beginning of a good thing for the Wadsquad, but that it was the beginning of the end with Slim.

No one was getting paid to be on the show – supposedly. But I saw so much money transfer that my head was spinning. I saw the promoter get some money, Paul gave me some money to give to Slim, and I saw Paul get a big envelope full of money. I could have sworn Paul said that this was going to be a charity event. Hell, I don't know, maybe they were donating one percent of the proceeds. All I know was that I didn't get anything except exposure for my group. Slim was on an ego trip again that night, but his walls were about to start tumbling down, and I saw it coming. Whenever we did a show in Detroit, I liked to bring my old college buddy Collin Love on. He is a big fella, and I like working with him because he doesn't get starstruck; he does what he's supposed to do. I was glad he was there that particular night, because whenever Slim and Kim were together and were drinking, there was always some drama. Kim was drinking and taking Vicodin at the same time, and her pupils were so dilated they were taking up her whole eyeballs. It was ridiculous. Kim was starting to trip out!

She was sitting on the floor. She was mad and crying, and she didn't know why. Her sister came over to me and said, "Kim's had too much to drink, too many drugs, she's mad at Slim, and she wants to drive home." I was like, "Look, y'all, don't start that shit tonight, please! Just be cool. Just calm down," because I knew it would just escalate. About an hour passed, and Kim and Slim's argument was getting worse. She was mad because she wasn't getting any attention; everyone was focusing on Slim Shady. Some people were used to this because it happened so frequently, and others were sick of it. Even members of his own crew started leaving. Unfortunately, I had to stay, along with my friend Collin. Kim was trying to drive home, but she was so drunk and high that she could hardly stand up. Things were getting ugly. Kim's sister gave me their car keys, and I told Kim and Slim that I would drive them home since they had been drinking and taking Vicodin.We would just come and pick up their truck tomorrow, which would be the best thing. Then Kim began her drunken protest – "You can't tell me what to do; you're not my father," blah, blah, blah. "I'm not trying to be your father, but if y'all go out driving in this condition, you will go to jail or someone will get hurt." I told Kim to think about Hailey, think about what was more important, her driving drunk or getting home safely. "You think about it and make your decision because I'm not going to say anything further on the topic." So, I walked away and left C-Love with them in the dressing room. I made a pit stop and came back, and all I saw was Kim attacking Slim, and C-Love trying to pull her off him.

Proof was trying to hold back Slim. I told Proof to get Kim out of there. In the process of him trying to do that, she hit Proof in the chin. Proof had seen this scene for the past ten years, and he was tired of it. He had enough of them fighting. Proof was tired of being in the middle. CLove tried to get Kim out of there, but she tried to slap him, so he was like, "Fuck this! I'm not getting involved in this domestic shit." I tried to get Slim away from her, and she pushed me from behind. I told her, "Don't ever put your hands on me. I don't get paid enough for this shit! You don't ever put your hands on me!" I told Slim, "If she puts her hands on me again, I'm going to act like I don't know her!" Kim got mad and stormed out. Slim was like, "Naz, go get her!" I said, "Look, she put her hands on me. If she wants to leave, let her leave," but I told C-Love to kind of trail her. He gave me a look that said he didn't expect to be doing all of this extra shit, but I told him to do it, and I would appreciate it as a favor. CLove and Kim's sister trailed her.They went out to the parking lot and lost C-Love.The story we got was that Kim punched her sister in the eye— again! Then Kim took the car keys and drove off.

Kim was now gone, driving drunk. She was gone literally and figuratively. She was high and drunk.We were trying to get Slim together, and he was worried about Kim, which was understandable because she was in no condition to drive. She was either going to kill somebody, be killed, or end up in jail. I told Slim I would take him home, but it would be better if he stayed at a hotel or over at my house because if he went home he would end up in jail because they would only get into another fight. He agreed. "Man, let's just go!" While Slim and I were in the parking lot, one of the groupies came up with this big-ass bag of pills, and that held us up for another ten minutes. Mark Labelle (Slim's road manager) politicked these pills for him. Then Slim said he was straight at that point, since he had the pills, and I was like, "Man, this shit never stops." He tried to put the pills under my car seat, and I was like, "Man, you better put that shit in your pocket because if we get pulled over I'm not getting caught up in that shit – that's a lot of pills." He said he would tell the police they were his if we got pulled over, but I was like, "Fuck that! Put that shit in the trunk," and he did.

On the drive home, Slim decided to spend the night at my house rather than go to his house, but my boy was throwing an unofficial after-party that we wanted to check out first. At one point, Paul found out about it and confronted me about it that night, but I nipped that in the bud quickly and told him not to ever confront me on some shit some-one else was doing. "That's my man's party, not mine." Paul was like,"Well, you tell him," and I cut him off again like, "Naw, here he is right here. If you have something to say to him, you tell him, and I suggest you handle business better next time," and I walked off. While we were in the car on the way home, Slim got a call on his cell phone from Kim's sister and, surprise, surprise – Kim had been arrested for drunk driving in Troy. She blew a 3.0 on the Breathalyzer.We had to go way out of our way to Troy to get her because she was locked up in the back of a police car. Slim convinced the police over the phone not to impound his car because he was on his way. I told Slim that the police knew who he was so not to agitate them and to just let them do all the talking, and we would get out of there.

Luckily, the police were fans of his, and everything worked out OK. The police told him that normally they impound the car, but since it was in his name they wouldn't, but if Kim was ever caught again driving drunk, they would take the car and her license because that would be her third time.They also told Slim that if she would have hit or killed somebody that he would end up broke because the car is in his name, and he would be held responsible.That blew Slim away.The police let us go, and all they wanted was a picture with Slim Shady and an autograph out of the deal. Slim ended up going back to the apartment. I thought about everything that had just happened and decided to go holler at my boys at the party anyway. My boy who threw the party wanted to know where Slim was, and I told him what happened. That was pretty much how my adventure with Slim and Kim ended that night.

November 27th

I called Slim's apartment to see what was going on. I found out that they hadn't yet released Kim, whom they had clocked going eighty mph in a twenty-mph zone, swerving, and it was a miracle that she hadn't killed herself or someone else. Pathetic.They also revoked her license indefinitely, and it was possible that she would have to serve some jail time. Slim was going to have to spend a lot of money, because he had hired a lawyer and was trying to keep her out of jail, at least until after Christmas. Kim is just a reckless person.You would think that Slim, being the wild hip-hop star, would be the reckless one. He did his share of crazy shit, but Kim was just outlandish. It was a bad reflection on him. Not only was his mother suing him, but also he was going to have to shell out twenty or thirty grand representing Kim in court, and Paul was controlling his money. Plus, Kim might still have to do some jail time.

Kim is going to AA meetings to show she's getting help, but how long is that going to last? Knowing Kim, she is still going to keep drinking and driving.Thinking back over all the past events that I witnessed, I wondered why Slim stayed with her in the first place. She would drive a normal man crazy. The biggest thing I fear for Slim is his life, because I fear that she is either going to kill him or he is going to kill her, or she is going to do something to make him go broke. I don't know if she realizes what she is doing, but she is doing it. I can recall one time in South Carolina on the Warped Tour when Slim flew Kim and a few of her family members out so they could enjoy themselves. He treated them real nice and did a lot more than he had to do for them.

At one point, we were loading up the bus and suddenly I saw Slim and Kim getting into this huge blowout fight. They had both been drinking, but they weren't overly drunk or anything. This wasn't caused by liquor, this fight stemmed from something else. I'm not quite sure what; all I knew was they were both fuming. He was sitting at a table with his legs up and his head against a mirror, and she was standing. He told her that he was going to send her home tomorrow and, as usual, she flipped the script and involved Hailey. She kept saying, "This is how you do your daughter? You're just going to send Hailey home??" She kept saying that over and over. She always did that to make him seem like the bad guy. She tried to twist everything and use Hailey against him. He really wanted to spend all the time in the world with Hailey, but not with Kim, and I don't blame him. The bitch is crazy! He was like, "Kim, you got to go, you got to get out of here.You are going home tomorrow." It got really ugly.

Slim was like, "Naz, will you get her out of here?" And I was like, "Man, I told you before that I don't like to get involved in this domestic shit, and if y'all can handle this between yourselves, I would very much prefer that." He was like, "Naz, she has to go!" So, everyone was looking at me to get her off the tour bus. There I was, trying to coax Kim off the bus, like, "Kim, we have to get on the road, you have to go." She was like, "I'm not leaving. This is all the time he wants to spend with his daughter," and I was like, "Kim, it's not that, it's you." She was steadily ranting and raving, and the whole scene was sick. I decided to go outside the bus and tell her cousins what was going on and that Gus, the tour manager, had arranged for them to leave tomorrow.We would give them some money if they wanted to stay longer, that they would definitely be taken care of, but Kim and Slim were getting into it. Slim was tired, and Kim was causing too many problems on this tour. Kim's relatives didn't like it, but they understood. I convinced one of Kim's cousins to come get Kim off the tour bus because I didn't like to get involved in the domestic aspect of the problem. She agreed, and by that time there were groupies gathering in front of the hotel, and they could hear everything being said. They were standing in awe because they were getting a real-life taste of what he talked about on his album. They were like, "Wow that's Hailey! That's Slim! That's Kim! Wow this is just like the album!!"

I managed to convince some people to leave, but some remained, staring. It was like some paparazzi shit. Kim's cousin tried—unsuccessfully —to get her to leave. Slim then stood up and said, "Kim, will you please leave?" and she used this moment as an opportunity to try to provoke him into a fight, saying, "Oh, you want to fight me now?" He just sat back down and said, "No, Kim, I don't want to fight you. I just want you to leave. I will call you tomorrow. I just don't want to go through this anymore." Suddenly, she was like "Fuck you, Marshall!" and slammed his head into the mirror – BAM!! He sprang up from the chair with his fists balled up, but he didn't hit her. I could tell he wanted to beat the shit out of her – and I wanted to help him – but he didn't hit her.

By this time, I was standing between them, and he was yelling at the top of his lungs for her to get off the bus, and she was trying to get at him even more. I was like,"OK, Kim, you've proven your point, it's time for you to go." So she reached around me and pushed his head with her finger. She was trying to irritate the hell out of him, and I know she was, but all he was trying to do was not catch a case. At this point, I was guiding Kim off the bus gently by her elbows, and she pushed me. I said, "C'mon, Kim, this is between you and your husband, not me and you. I'm trying to make the situation better, and you are trying to make it worse," etc. She was like, "Fuck you, Naz. He's not a good father. All you guys do is what he tells you to do. You guys all kiss his ass!!" I was like, "Kim, I'm trying not to hear that. You have put your hands on me now, and I am trying not to hear that!" I stepped outside, because trying to be a gentleman to a total bitch had made me reach my threshold of tolerance. She is the type of woman who wants you to put your hands on her. She wants to fight.

Finally, she decided to get off the bus. She was making a big scene in front of his fans, saying how he's not a good father and he didn't want his daughter on the tour bus with him. She was really trying to demean his character. They gave me like $500 to give to her if she decided to stay, so I took it up to her room, and she said to me, "You know, Naz, all you guys do is kiss his ass. He's always wrong, but you guys all kiss his ass." I told her, "First of all, you don't know anything about me, because I took a leave from my job to do this, so when I quit working for him I have a job to go to. So, I don't have to kiss anybody's ass. Second of all, you have got to be the biggest idiot I have ever seen. You have a man out here busting his ass making money, taking care of you. He acknowledges his daughter, he takes care of his daughter, he gives you the world, and he takes care of you and your whole family. You don't show him any support whatsoever. All you do is come out here and bust his balls. I don't know what he does to you when we are not around to make you act this way. He is trying; you aren't even trying. You don't even try to support him. You don't even try to let him be the man because you are such a bully. You need to realize what you've got and stop being so foolish. I know marriage isn't easy because I'm married. But there are a million women out here that would love to be in your shoes, and you want to give all that up? You need to think about that. I'm out."

Honestly, I hope the two of them can be friends if their marriage fails because right now they are on two different pages. I refer to a passage in the Bible, Ecclesiastes Chapter 7 Verse 17, which states, "Do not be overly wicked nor be foolish. Why should you die before your time?"

November 29th, Back to Business

Slim called me and told me he wanted to go get his gun registered and get his gun permit. I told him, "Cool, because I need to check on some of my personal gun permits as well." I took my older son along with me, and we picked Slim up from his mother-in-law's house. Slim and my son were laughing together, and my son said to me, "Daddy, you have a belly and you are bald headed." I said, "Yes, son, I do have a belly and I am bald headed. My father has a belly and is bald headed, too. It runs in the family. Therefore, when you grow up you will have a belly and be bald headed, as well." He just stood there with this dumbfounded look on his face. I guess he was trying to imagine himself bald headed with a belly, and everyone in the place got a kick out of that. My son didn't think that was funny at all; he didn't like that too much. But I thought it was funny, and so did everyone else. Anyway, we were in this place getting Slim's concealed weapons permit, and I didn't feel comfortable because he hadn't gotten Paul's permission. I knew somehow that it would come back on me, since Paul was his manager. I told Slim I don't go behind peoples' backs, that's not how I do business, but I

DJ Head shows off one of his many fat joints! London, England.

guess he felt that since he was home and Paul was in New York that he could do some things on his own. I told him,"OK, but when Paul has questions about it, I am just letting you know that you deal with him because all I did was bring you here, and me and him are already on different pages." He was like, "OK, no problem."When it came time for him to pay for his permit, he didn't have any checks on him, just like I figured he wouldn't. That's why I had made it a point to grab my checkbook. Slim told to me that he needed a check because Paul had all of that stuff in New York, so I wrote out the check for him. He took the test, and they told him it would be few months before he received his permit.

After that, I dropped him off at the studio, where he and D-12 were doing some recording. They said they would take him home, and I told them that was OK because there was enough of them where they could handle it if something jumped off. I took my son to the movies, then went home and gathered all my receipts from money I spent that I needed to be reimbursed for. Half my cell phone bills were usually Slim's calls. Basically, my cell phone was his cell phone because he always lost his cell phone. My last cell phone bill was shut off with an amount due of $1,221, all that needed to be paid to keep it on was $650. When Slim talked, he talked like it was a house phone. I was supposed to be reimbursed for all Slim's calls, as well as any incoming or outgoing calls concerning business. I gathered all of my receipts and my cell phone bill and sent them overnight Federal Express to Slim's accountant, Bruce Secondorf.

The next day, I received a call from him stating that they weren't going to pay for my whole cell phone bill. I explained to them that that wasn't my whole bill, which was half my cell phone bill. They said that they weren't going to pay that, that they needed an itemized list, etc. I told them that what they have is what the phone company sent me. It was a shut-off notice, and they didn't send an itemized list. I explained to them that half of those calls were made by Slim.We went back and forth about it, and I got off the phone pissed off because they said they weren't going to pay it. Then I got another call later on regarding the check for the gun permit. The secretary said Paul wanted to know what that was all about before they paid it, and I told her to tell Paul to call Slim to find out about it. She was like, "Well, we can't pay you any money until we know," and I was like, "Whatever. Just have Paul talk to Slim and pay me my money."

Paul still tried to come to me with this middleman shit, and I again told him he had to talk to Slim about the permit. I told him the same thing I had told Slim about the permit situation, that I wasn't dealing with Paul on that.The next day, I got another call from Paul about the cell phone bill. I told him the same thing I told Slim's accountant. Slim was responsible for half because he didn't have a phone while we were in California, and he always used mine. Paul said they weren't going to pay it, and I was like, "What the hell do you mean you aren't going to pay it? Slim made the calls and y'all owe me that money." We went back and forth, and he said he had to talk to Slim about it first. I was like, "Whatever. Do what you got to do. If y'all would have set up a petty cash fund for Slim like I told you this would not even be an issue." All in all, the total correct amount that I should have gotten reimbursed was $850, but I only got $450, which wasn't even enough to cover my phone bill. My phone ended up getting shut off for about a week.

Then the next day, I got a call from Slim, and I thought he might need me for something, so I was like, "What's up man?"Then he said,"We got to talk. Paul says you're trying to get more money out of me, man." I was like, "What are you talking about?" He was like, "He says you are trying to get me to pay your cell phone bill." I explained to him, the same as before, that it was only half, and he was responsible for it. He was like, "Man, I didn't know you were charging me, man." I said, "Slim, I don't make money like you do, so all that talking you did to your girls and shit I need to be reimbursed for." He was like, "What about all the times we went out and I paid for your dinner, man?" and I was like, "What about all the times we went out and I paid for everything? But look, I'm not about to go tit for tat with you over this shit.What is your point? We never had a problem over this before, so why now? You called me with this shit. Paul is trying to make it seem like I'm trying to steal from you. I told you, I don't have to steal from you. Before I met you I had nice shit, and after I leave you I'm going to have nice shit. Plus, if I'm going to steal from you, I'm damn sure going to steal more than $600.You've got millions! You need to get Paul out of your head because he is brainwashing you, and if anyone is stealing from you it's him. Everyone doesn't have fat bank accounts like you and Paul. This issue is petty to y'all, but it's serious to me. I spent that money out of my own pockets, and I need to be reimbursed. If that's going to be a problem, then you need to let me know right now. But you are calling me accusing me of stealing, so what is this, are you saying you are firing me? Is that what this is?" He was like, "Na, man, I'm just saying do you like your job?" And I said, "What does that shit mean, don't you get taken care of? Why would you ask me something like that? I take care of you as if you were my own son." He was like, "That doesn't have anything to do with anything." I said, "Yes, it does matter. I take care of you, Slim. After all I do for you, you call me with this bullshit, man. I never got to steal from you man. Y'all are getting on my bad side now accusing me of this shit. That night when Kim got arrested and you were drunk, Paul gave me three grand to give to you, and I didn't steal any of that, and every time I held money for you, I had receipts accounted for.You need to watch Paul because he is fucking with your brain. I know that's your boy, but he has you thinking that everyone around you is stealing from you, and that's some bullshit. He's making everyone else look like the bad guy while he's the fucking villain. I don't have to steal from nobody, and I never have because I have always had."

We continued to go back and forth and he said, "I talked to Bruce, too." I was like, "Yeah, and?" And he said, "You are the only one keeping up trouble." I said, "Keeping up trouble? How's that?" and he was like, "You are always complaining." I was like, "Look, any time there's money missing out of my check I need to know why. I need to have those questions answered, man. When they take money out of your check they are supposed to list on there why they took the money out, and they don't do that, man. Y'all mutha fuckas got millions man, I'm just making this little $1,300 a week, and y'all call here insulting me like I'm trying to steal from y'all." So he was like, "Well, we just wanted to know if you like your job, man," and I was like, "Yeah, I like my job, but that doesn't mean you can call here and accuse me of shit and insult me. If y'all are going to fire me then do what you got to do. I can walk away from this job. Just let me know. Paul is your man; he doesn't have shit to do with me. I would appreciate it if you would keep him out of your head when it comes to me because he obviously has something against me. I intimidate him because I am an intelligent big black man with my own connections and I don't ask y'all for shit. I don't like the way he treats me, as a matter of fact. He won't take my phone calls at his office or the cell phone; he only talks to me on the SkyTel pager. I think that's why he bought it because he is scared to talk to me for some reason. I am closer to you than he is. I am on the road with you all the time and you let him get into your head about me? That's real fucked up, man.You need to reevaluate that. I see where I stand now, man."

Then Slim said I was tripping and brought up the fact–one I didn't like–that we might have to do something in December, and I was like,"You are damn right. I have been on the road with you all for eight months, and you promised me the whole month of December off, and I made plans with my family.You already fucked up this weekend for me that I was supposed to have off because you have to do something with Dre." He was like,"Well, shit comes up man." I was like,"Well, I can't plan shit because y'all's word doesn't mean shit.You tell me one thing, then you do another. I got guys that'll cover you who you are familiar with. You've seen these guys work. If they are good enough for Dre and Funkmaster Flex, they are damn sure good enough to work for you, so what's the problem?" He was like, "Well, they ain't you. I feel like if some shit jumps off, they can't cover me." I said, "Come on, now. These guys are cops, they are professionals, and they have been in the business way longer than I have. I know they would do top-of-the-line work." He was like, "Naw, man. They aren't you, man. I want you there. You always get to be with your family." I said, "Look, my family comes first. You are not first, my family is first and foremost." And he said again, "Well, we just want to know if you like your job, man." I said, "Look, if you are going to fire me then let me know so I can call GM and tell them I will be at work in the morning, because I don't have time Shady Bizzness 129 129 for this shit, man. Y'all have thoroughly insulted me today." He was like, "Alright then," and I said, "Alright, I'm out. Peace."

And that is how that conversation ended.

7

THE BEEF IS ON!

The cost of fame is too expensive for my taste.The next day after the discussion with Slim, I felt like we had both cleared the air. My decision was made because I was finished working with Slim and Paul.They treated me like I was a slave and as if I had nothing else better to do. I basically called my job and told them that I was going to be coming back at the end of the year. I interviewed for a promotion within the union at GM because that was the best thing for me. I had seen the disturbing side of the industry, not just with Slim but in the entire industry. In the music business, people acted as if they owned you, and nobody owned me. It was their fault that they didn't have a contract with me, and if we had a contract none of these problems would have occurred.We both would have been legally bound to our expectations and our duties. But that's their loss and nothing but gain for me. It gave me time to spend with my wife and kids and try to get myself together because I gained everything I could from working with Paul and Slim, and I felt as though there were nothing else for me to gain.

Paul and Slim weren't going to offer my group a deal on their label, and it wasn't because my group wasn't any good, but that their pride wouldn't allow them to ask me for anything. So I did my interview, and everything went very well, and I'll be getting the position. Ironically, on the way home from my interview I noticed a package on my front porch. It was the platinum plaque awarded to me for my contribution to the success of the Slim Shady Tour. I wasn't sure whether to throw it away, sell it, or what, but I knew I wasn't putting it on display at my house. I wasn't going to put it up until I saw something positive come from the situation. Meanwhile, I was trying to adjust to the so-called flexible month of December. I was supposed to get time off to spend with my family, but it was difficult to plan because every time something came up on the tour, like when Slim was supposed to record a song or something, it was canceled. I had to cancel plans that I already made because I was told that I was going to have the whole month of December off. My backup help, Rock and Noel, had the same problem with the planning and canceling that occurred in the month of December, and they missed out on a lot of money because of this. This is where they began to see what I was going through working security for Paul and Slim, and how Paul had no regard for other people's time or money. Paul and Slim always acted like everyone's bank account was on their level, but unfortunately that's not the case. I always told Paul that he needed to understand that playing with people's money and time was dangerous. It got to the point where Rock and Noel would come to me and say, "Naz, what is Paul going to do?" I told them that I was supposed to be the one running security, but Paul kept intervening because he wanted to be a control freak. Any questions they had regarding the pay, reservations, and commitment should be directed to Paul. All I could do is tell them when we were supposed to be leaving, but they keep canceling everything. Then, Paul came to me and told me that we were going to be doing New Year's Eve in New York.

I really didn't like this idea because so many plans had been made and then canceled that month, I really had no quality time to spend with my family. I couldn't take any vacations with my family or visit family members in other states because my plans kept being rearranged. It was just a big mess. The closer and closer it got to January, the more antsy I got because I was ready to go back to work. Working with Slim and Paul, I was being totally disrespected as a businessman. They had an "either you do as I say or you're out" attitude. In January, I went back to work and got the rest of my retainer money. If they would have gone anywhere, of course, I would have had to go as well, but I was just trying to get through the month of December. Some other things were going on as well. My wife had come down with pneumonia and was supposed to check in to the hospital, and I had no plans to leave her in that condition. They wanted to keep her when she went in, but she didn't want to be in the hospital for the holidays so she didn't stay, but she was pretty

Ladies love lip-locking! Now that's a tongue twister.

sick. That helped me to make my decision as well. I told Paul the day after Christmas on his answering machine that we needed to talk, and it couldn't wait.

He called me while he was in a meeting with Slim and D-12, and I told him that I needed more money because my CCW permits came in, and I was more qualified, and that I needed more control over security or I wasn't getting on the plane the next day. He told me that he had no intentions of paying me any more money than I was already getting. I told him that it was nice working with him and Slim, and that since all my requests and proposals weren't respected, the relationship had to be cut. I told him that I was a businessman and that I wasn't being respected as such. I wished them much success and said I would continue to buy their records but that I could no longer work for the minimal wages that they were paying. I gave them until midnight that night to change my mind because I could go back to work and make the same amount of money that they were paying me. Paul responded, "Well, how are you going to wait until the last minute when we are supposed to fly out to California at noon tomorrow to shoot the 'Still Dre' video?" I gave him a taste of his own medicine. I said, "Well Paul, everything in this business is last minute, so get used to it. Again, you have until midnight tonight to change my mind because I can't do this under these conditions."

That was a big step for me, and I felt good about it. I didn't have any regrets. I went upstairs, and I gave my wife the news that Paul didn't care to meet the total amount of money I wanted, which was $300 a day. Comparatively, this wasn't a lot of money, because some guys get $700 or more a day, up to a thousand, and there I was getting $185. I was glad I had made my decision. I went downstairs and got on the Internet, and lo and behold one of the villains from the past e-mailed me—DT. He was basically on a positive note, just asking how are you doing hope everything is going well; I remember a lot of good things about you. Now, how unexpected was that? I just resigned from Paul and Slim, and DT happens to send me e-mail. He was one of my biggest nemeses on the tour when it first started, and now he was trying to be my friend. It was an eerie feeling because it almost seemed like DT knew what was going on. I e-mailed him back, letting him know that everything was cool and that I was just getting ready for the New Year. We corresponded over the next few days, but I didn't tell him the news.

The first person I told was Gus, who commended me and reassured me that I had done the right thing. They screwed Gus over financially, too. I called Rowe and told him, and, of course, I told Rock and Noel. I sent the rest of the people I had met and worked with an e-mail, letting them know that it was nice to work with them and that I hoped to talk to them in the future. That was basically how I closed out my resignation because I didn't want people to hear anything except for the truth first. I had resigned, not been fired, and it felt good. About an hour after I resigned, I got a call from Proof. He told me that I fucked Paul and Slim up with that news. He said it was right, because they were acting like big shots at the meeting. I told Proof that was how they always acted. Proof said the first thing out of Paul's mouth was, "Damn, I didn't get a chance to fire him." I knew that is what Paul wanted to do. He wanted to fire me and drag my name through the mud. He wanted to have something negative on me so bad he could taste it. I thought that I ended it on a good note, but I found out otherwise later.

December 27th

Slim and Paul flew out to California, and I made preparations to go back to work. I didn't feel any regrets, much to my surprise. I was happy to be back with my family and friends. I was thankful that I wasn't a materialistic person because I didn't get so caught up in the hype that it hurt me to leave it. I owed it all to my upbringing, to my mom for instilling a good sense of morals and to my father for always being straight up with me about life. That's the one thing I had over Paul and Slim. They had no father figures. Slim never knew his father, and Paul's father left his mother when he was young. I know things happen, but I was a different type of man. I was a better man than both of them put together. The two of them didn't equal half of me, and it showed, and they knew it. And they say that black fathers aren't any good! I am here to tell you that I have the best dad in the world, and the most loving mom, and because of that I am a good dad and a great man, all blessed by God. That is something that Paul and Slim didn't understand and could never take from me. But they did manage to affect me financially.

December 30th

I had no idea that this day was going to be what it was. This day made my whole entire year the worst I ever had. I almost lost everything. I almost lost my wife, my kids, my freedom, and my religion. What went down was a shock, a harsh reality. It was like being thrown in a pot of hot water while you are asleep. You wonder how the hell you got there. I got a call from the bank where my wife works. Her boss called her and told her that the checks we cashed had a stop put on them. The three grand Christmas bonus had been cashed eight days ago. We had already spent that and invested it. Also, my retainer check had been canceled. I immediately went through the roof when my wife told me this. Her boss asked her what we were going to do about the money. We had to put some money in our account to keep it out of negative status, which greatly inconvenienced us. All of this because stupid-ass Paul and Slim couldn't handle the fact that I didn't want to work for them anymore.They did this out of spite. Automatically, right off the bat, I snapped. I went off. I honestly wasn't thinking about my wife and my kids. All I could think about was all of the work that I did for these guys, that I left my family to work for them, that I stood in front of Death Row and other dangerous situations and put my life on the line. I thought about my Christmas bonus, which was short as it was because it was supposed to have been five grand, but it was only three grand. They canceled the check eight days after the check was cashed out of spite just because I didn't want to work for them.

The first thing I did was go down to my basement, and I loaded up my clip. I put on my bulletproof vest. I loaded my second clip and put it on my belt. I grabbed my tear gas and my baton because at this point somebody was about to get their ass beat. Someone was about to get dealt with. I totally got beyond myself. I allowed the devil to step in and take over my whole mind-set. I was gone; I snapped just that quickly without even thinking. I stopped and thought and said, "Well, let me call Paul," because I was about to go out on a manhunt. The part that hurt me the most was that I had been loyal to them throughout the entire duration. I thought about all of the physical and mental sacrifices I made dealing with these fools, and this was the thanks I got! I deserved both of those checks – plus some. I felt disrespected and punked out and like they were trying to play games with my life. All I could see was red.

Then I realized that that's what these guys were all about – paper gangsters, straight bitches. They knew they couldn't beat me mentally or physically, so they played the only game they could: big bank take little bank. And I must say, they got me that time.They pushed a button that no one ever pushed before because these boys had me ready to lay some people down. I called Paul, and of course he didn't answer. Unthinkingly, I left him a voice mail. I left a verbal threat to do some damage. Not a very wise choice! Ironically, I had turned into a person I didn't like. I was doing something that I said I wasn't going to do and that was give in to the devil by chasing the money. They used the money as an object for me to chase after. For me, it wasn't just the money; it was the loyalty I had given and the lack of respect that I received. It was a ton of things, and everything I had put up with over the months, all the positions I passed up at my job, missing out on my newborn son's first year, and a lot more.

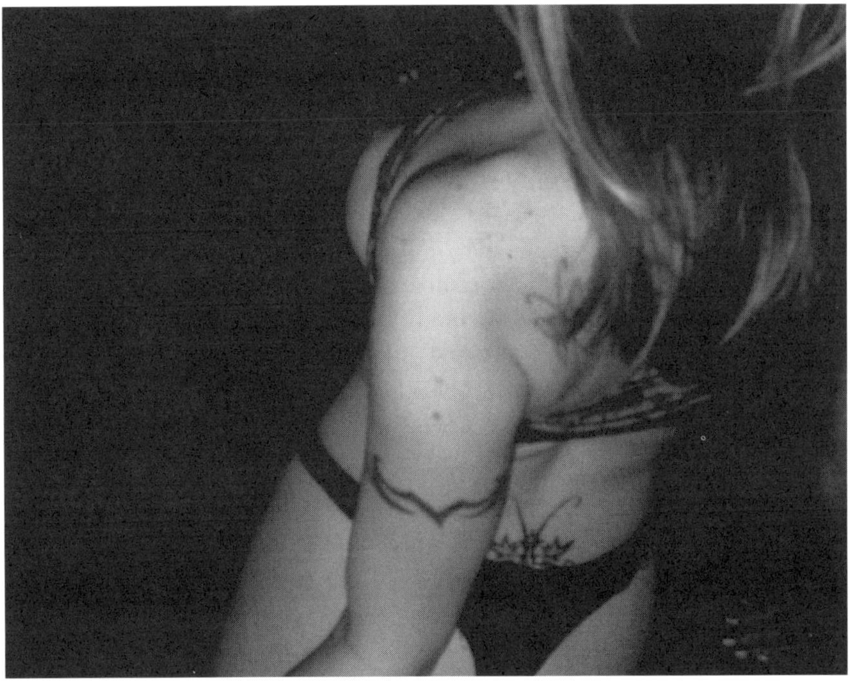

Lap dance, table top, get it! Get it! Don't stop!

These are all the things I could see, and all I could think about was hurting these guys in a way that their mothers would feel. Paul didn't answer the phone, so I left a message saying that they knew exactly what they had done and had taken money from me that was rightfully mine, and, "Just because I am a family man, don't think that I won't do something to your ass because I will. The best way to correct this is to give me my fuckin' money back. It's very ironic that y'all hired me to be y'all's bodyguard, but now you have to hire somebody to protect y'all from me. I am not bullshitting, man. I want my money. You will never be able to go anywhere treating people like this, and you won't have to worry about Death Row because the wrath that I'm going to put on your ass, you will never forget. You and Slim. That's not a threat, that's a promise. Now, give me my fuckin' money back, and I mean that shit."

Right after I left Paul this message on his cell phone, I called Slim, and I was still madder than a mutha fucka. His wife,Kim, answered his cell phone and handed it to Slim, who came on the line sounding coy and acting like he didn't know what was going on, just like he always does. He knew damn well what was going on. I questioned him about pulling my money, and he said I didn't do shit the whole month of December, and it was my fault. I told him that I called him daily to let him know that I was available. Paul got into Slim's head once again, making him betray the people who supported him the most. I told him I resigned, and it was strictly a business decision, but they made it personal. He said, "Fuck you, Naz," and I said, "Oh, it's like that? Well fuck you, too." He was like,"Well, what are you going to do? I got a gun." And I was like, "What the fuck do you mean what am I going to do? Have you forgotten whom you are talking to? I got guns! You hired me to protect you because you couldn't do it yourself. Man, please get the fuck out of here with that shit. I'm trying to get my money back." He kept testing me and challenging me to do something or make a move, and I kept telling him all I wanted was my money back and that I was making the phone call to avoid coming over there. He was ranting and raving on the phone trying to be hard, and I told him I was on my way there. He was like, "Whatever!" and hung up the phone. Little did I know that Paul and Slim were plotting. At this point I was really mad as hell. I wasn't sure where Paul was, but I knew that Slim was home.

Since I had been his bodyguard, I knew his every move before he even made it. I knew where he hung at, ate at, recorded at, lived at, and partied. At any given moment, I could find him. I was thinking, Man, this guy don't know who he is fucking with. He must think he is dealing with some type of punk or something. I was outside pacing and mad, just fuming, and my wife was trying to get me to come back into the house because I have a family, but I wasn't trying to hear that shit. All I was thinking of was hurting Paul and Slim the way I was hurting. It wasn't a hurt from the money; it was a hurt from betrayal. I was the realest person Slim has ever had around him. I didn't ask him for shit or want for nothing. I watched his back and cared about him. He fucked me, and he helped Paul fuck me. Paul, being the big bitch that he is, knew that the only way he could deal with me was through Slim. He never could deal with me one on one. That's why he wouldn't accept my calls and wouldn't talk to me. I intimidated him.

I had all these voices going through my head. I was hearing my father telling me not to mess up my name – "You've got kids! You've got a wife." I was feeling totally belittled and discouraged and feeling a lot of anguish. I wasn't trying to hear what God had to say or what my wife had to say. I wanted to handle it my way. I wasn't trying to hear what my father had to say. In fact, I was deaf to anything that was going to help me better this situation. I had become a monster. I had become the person that I was working for, and that's sad. The industry had gotten the best of me.

Little did I know that voicemail on Paul's cell phone would alter my life. I decided to just get in my truck and drive. I still maintained my thoughts of hurting Paul and Slim, but rather than act on those thoughts, I went shopping to occupy some time and to ease my mind.The way I was feeling, I would have gone over to Slim's house and literally killed that boy. I listened to some gospel music to help me to rebuke the devil, because I had become so evil and enraged at that point that I wasn't trying to hear anything. I felt like I had turned my back on God and my family. I wanted it to be my revenge.

I asked God why he let them treat me this way, and I realized that it wasn't God's fault. It was my fault. Because once they turned me down the first time I gave them a proposal, I should have resigned then. But you live and you learn, and one thing I learned from that situation is that if people don't take you seriously, then you have to show them just how serious you are.

After I finished shopping and calmed myself down, I had come to my senses. I said to myself that the conversation Slim and I had on the phone was real fucked up and that he and I had some history now.We should be able to sit down and resolve this like men. I had come to a conclusion that I didn't want to take this into the New Year; I wanted to start Y2K off right. I reluctantly headed over to his house hearing two voices: one telling me to stop over at Slim's house and the other telling me not to. I realized that I probably should not have gone over there, but the problem had to be confronted. I went over there, and I was still wearing my bulletproof vest and carrying my .40 cal with two fully loaded clips,my baton, and my tear gas. I went to his house ready to talk with a sensible mind, but I knew not to underestimate Slim because he could be high or drunk, as usual. He can be very stupid when he's impaired.

When I got out of my truck at his house, his truck wasn't there. I went up to his door and knocked softly, with my other hand in my pocket on my .40 caliber, just in case! After I knocked, I heard everyone in his mother-in-law's house scrambling, panicking, screaming, and hollering. It was obvious that they knew that Slim and I were beefing from our phone conversation. I heard Kim saying, "Oh, my God, he's here! He's going to do something to us! Call Slim!" Slim was hiding out at a friend's house around the corner to avoid seeing me. I told him I was coming to see him on some street shit, but since I had calmed down, I was only there to talk to him. But if he wanted to get into some gangster shit we could have gone that route, too. Unlike Slim, I own CCW permits. All my shit was legal, and I had a right to defend myself.When Kim finally decided to open the door, she was the nicest she's ever been to me. She was crying. "Naz, what do you want? Slim said you were going to kill us – you were going to kill Hailey and me and we don't want any problems. You guys need to quit this!" I said, "Look, Kim, I came over here to talk because the conversation Slim and I had on the phone was real fucked up. Since we have history, we should be able to talk this out."

She was like, "Well, he's not here," and I said to her, "No problem. Just give him the message and tell him to call me so that we can iron this out." I was trying to be a bigger man and do this the right way. It wasn't easy for me to do, because some real grimy thugs would have taken his family hostage or killed somebody for fucking with their money and livelihood. At the point when I got out of the truck, I felt like I had allowed the Lord to come back in. I wasn't a fool, and I wasn't about to allow myself to be locked away for thirty years from my sons. I went over there to be logical and civilized, but if he wanted to be stupid, he was going to get dealt with. I was going to be leaving in one piece. After giving Kim the message, I saw Slim pulling up around the corner in his truck. I was like, "Oh, there he is right there," and she was like, "Well, Naz, be careful, he's got a gun!" I said, "I am not worried about that because so do I! I was loyal to him and I just want to talk to him about getting my money back that he owes me." She was like, "You should get out of here! You should leave!" I told her I could take care of myself, but she still said, "You should leave!" so I said, "OK." I saw Slim sitting at the corner in his truck like a coward, because I could have been doing anything to his wife.

Showdown

When he saw me walking to my truck, he decided to pull up. I showed him my hands as a peace treaty. I told him that the phone conversation was sour and that we needed to handle this like men. He was red in the face and high and obviously nervous. I said we should be able to handle this without Paul interfering. He wasn't listening. He was panicking and yelling, "What are you doing here?" and accusing me of trying to do something to his family. He was like, "Naz, I got a gun, and I'll shoot you!" I was like, "I don't give a fuck about that. I am the one who took you to apply for the CCW permit, if you haven't forgotten!" He told me to get off his property, and I was like, "This isn't even your property, this is your mother-in-law's property.What you and Paul did to me was illegal anyway. I just came to talk to you in a civilized manner. Again, how can I get my money? Let's do this without Paul being in the picture. Now, how can I get my money? Because I need my loot!" He was like, "Fuck you, Naz! Get off my property!" and he was just getting louder and louder and more nervous because we were the only two people outside at this point in an allwhite neighborhood. I put my hand back in my pocket on my gun. He saw that what he was saying to me wasn't bothering me at all. That was making him more nervous. He was getting louder, to draw the attention of potential witnesses. His neighbors started to come outside, and the louder he got, the quieter I got.The entire neighborhood saw him acting a fool. He was so frantic; he wasn't trying to hear me out. I just said, "Man, you are not scaring me," and at this time he decided to pull up his shirt and brandish his weapon. I said, "Oh it's like that, huh?" And he was like, "Yeah, the beef is on, nigga." And I was like, "Oh, I'm a nigga now, so it's like that." I slowly started easing my gun out of my coat pocket.

At that moment, I noticed Kim and Hailey on the porch crying, and that startled me back to reality. I thought about my family. Then I realized how it would look, being the only black guy in this all-white neighborhood with an exposed firearm, legal or not. When all these neighbors had congregated, I decided to leave. I said, "Slim, I love you, man. I loved you like a brother, and I don't appreciate the foul treatment." I told him I came to him to talk. I held him down and looked out for him like he was my own son, and this is the way he wanted to act. I told him to get Paul out of his head, because he had him brainwashed. I walked slowly to my truck. I could see all of his neighbors watching to see what the commotion was about. I could see that he was hurt, because I was hurt; I am a big enough man to say that my feelings were hurt. It was sad that we had reached this point. I didn't come over on any storm trooper shit. I came to talk. He escalated this to a level where it looked like I was the bad guy. I was glad I didn't pull my gun, because I would have had to take his life. Kim and Hailey saved his life that day, whether he knows it or not. I saw the twenty-to-one ratio of whites to blacks, and this one black guy would have been doing some jail time. I decided to leave. I told him that he would be hearing from my lawyer the next time he heard from me. I drove away at about five miles per hour so the witnesses couldn't say I sped off. That day the Lord was with us both because it could have been worse. I dread thinking about it.

I replayed that scene in my head and tried to determine whether my moves had been wise or not. The one thing that kept coming to my mind was Slim's last words to me. He said, "Naz, I thought you were my friend, man. I thought we were friends. You let me go out to California all by myself, and them muthafuckas could have got me! That ain't loyalty. I thought you was my friend!"That's how I knew he was hurt, too. I told him I was his friend but that he was taking it to the next level now. I decided to call the police to see if I could file a police report for him brandishing a weapon, not to get him locked up but just to have something on him so that he could know what it was like to feel uncomfortable about a situation. Little did I know that he and Paul had plotted using the phone message I made earlier that day. I found that out from the police department. They asked me if I was Byron, and they told me to go back over to Slim's house because they just sent a car over there, and they needed to ask me some questions. I was like, "Naw, I told you the man just brandished a weapon and verbally threatened me. I'm not going back over there, but what I will do is come in there and file a police report." They were like, "OK."We both stayed in the suburbs which were 90 percent white, with their share of racial incidents, and I definitely got my share that day.

The first thing I did after I got off the phone with the police was go home, doing the speed limit. I went in the basement and took my weapons off and took off my vest, and I was tripping on what all had happened. I regretted ever meeting this guy. This shit turned into something that I really didn't have time to deal with. I wondered what lie Slim and Paul told on me. I told my wife that I was going to the police station to file a police report and why. She was tripping out, too. She said the sad part was that Slim was probably feeling guilty, because it wasn't his doing, it was Paul's. I got to the police station, and the police officers automatically took Slim's side and didn't want to hear my side of the story. They said they weren't going to let me file a police report. I told them that they were violating my civil rights and that I would be back with my lawyer. They told me basically to do what I had to do and that Slim and Paul called them on a three way and filed a police report.They got a personal protection order based on the conversation I had with Slim and on the message I left on Paul's voice mail. They lied and said I threatened to kill Slim's wife and child. I admit, I threatened both Slim and Paul and made promises about what would happen if I didn't get my money, but I didn't involve their families—that was some bullshit. I now had a restraining order for me to stay away from Paul and Slim. Paul's bitch-ass was in New York. And if the beef was on like Slim said, then why did he need a restraining order? And I couldn't make a police report, so it was their word against mine. All the neighbors and Slim's family were involved, and with Paul being a lawyer, he brought Slim's wife and kids into it to hem me up. Slim bought into it even though he knew I didn't say that shit.

I went from being employed to being a criminal. And these white police officers believe this shit! And they violated my rights by not allowing me to file a police report. They said he committed no crime because it was his house. I told them that it was his mother-in-law's house, and they said that since he had that address on his driver's license, that made it his house. I told them that he broke three laws. Number one: No permit for carrying a concealed weapon. Number two: He had a concealed weapon in his car. Number three: He brandished a weapon and made a threat and asked them what they were going to do about it. They still wouldn't let me file a police report. I told them I would be back with my lawyer because this was obviously a black vs. white issue. They said, "Well, you are a big guy," and I said, "Being big has nothing to do with this, because if the shoe were on the other foot and I did any of those three things, I would be put in jail because I am black. Y'all know this, so now the whole thing is racial." I felt like I did when I was at Olivet College when a brother was accused of something he didn't do. Now I was dealing with white trash and a Jew. It seemed like every time I trusted someone outside of my race, it blew up in my face. I was very disappointed in Paul and Slim for stooping to a level lower than I had ever seen any white man stoop to.

They fabricated a lie saying that I was going to kill Kim and Hailey. I never threatened to kill anyone in my message, but they knew that was the only way they could get something on me to drag my name through the mud. I went twenty-nine years with a clean record until I met these two idiots, now I am a stalker and a killer. But I was their bodyguard to begin with! I still say they brought this situation on themselves because they were shady in handling their business. I didn't cause this, I was part of the solution, and they made it racial. Just one more lie starts a racial incident.They won the battle with the money, but I was going to win the war. Rather than take their lives, I was going to expose them for what they were. They said they were not prejudiced, but they didn't do anything to prove that. They showed themselves to be no different than any other white person who lies about blacks to shut them down. They can't stop me, though, even though they did tarnish my name. I am not going to let anybody threaten me anyway. But when it's white against black, and with Paul being a lawyer, the attitude is "white is right."

My rights were violated, and since I couldn't even file a police report, all I could do was hire a lawyer.

Time to Reflect

Decisions, decisions, decisions. I have realized that there is no such thing as a clean break. I felt really defeated. I couldn't get any money— and I damn sure couldn't get any justice. What could I get? I got a good lawyer.That's what I did. I postponed my return to work to take care of my legal matters. I had to think like Paul to figure out how

The crew hanging out in Paris, France.

to get next to Paul and Slim. I knew Slim's mom was suing him using Jeffrey Fieger (Dr. Kevorkian's attorney), so I decided to call his office. I went and talked to one of his associates in person, and it was like a blessing in disguise because this gentleman had a lot of connections. When I first called this attorney and told him the situation, the first thing out of his mouth was that he knew Paul. I told him at that point that I couldn't fuck with him. Then he said that he just knew who he was and that he had been in the business a long time and was also an entertainment lawyer. He said that he had an opportunity to manage Eminem, but at the time he had too much on his plate to do it.

Paul went to him pumping him for info, and he said he knew all about Paul. I told him the situation and that they owed me some money. I told him the whole story and why I didn't want to work for them anymore. The attorney was surprised that I had a label and groups, and he told me he was once a promoter for Universal, and we hit it off right off the bat. I went home and evaluated the situation, and I realized that the Lord really does work in mysterious ways. He was a criminal and civil and entertainment lawyer. He had met Paul and knew he was an asshole. The next time we spoke, we found out that the lawyer for the other side, Neil, was his best friend. I couldn't believe that. Mike called Neil right there on the phone, and they were talking back and forth about the case.

I was a little uncomfortable with it, with the two lawyers being friends and all, but I figured if my man could get my money back for me then I would use him. If it got dirty and grimy, I would just have to switch attorneys if my man got too friendly with this other guy. I kind of just sat back and observed things. He got off the phone, and as he continued to talk to me, he stated that he and Slim's attorney were Jews. I immediately thought I was done because one thing I can say about Jews is that they stick together—they are a unit—and I didn't want that. On this occasion, I wanted them to fight, for my sake, to get my money back and to get my name clean. Mind you, at this point I didn't want to sue Slim or Paul. I just wanted to get my name clean, get the five grand that they owed me, and get the protection order dropped. That's all I cared about, and that way I could move on with my life. I took a week off work to get this together, as far as the lawyer gathering all the information that he needed from me. Basically, this attorney and I were talking about two things at once: this case and the music business. I told him that the music business was on hold now because this was about my life and my name. I wanted my name cleared and the money that they owed me, and he understood that. The attorney for the other side was gung ho and being a total asshole. He acted like he had something to prove because he was defending a celebrity, and he wanted to put all his balls into it.

So my attorney told me that this could go one of two ways.The quieter of the two appealed to me because I didn't want the publicity to be a burden on my family. Paul also lied on his personal protection order, stating that I threatened one of his assistants, as well, which was an absolute fabrication.The attorney and I learned a lot about each other and the roles that we would have to play in this case. I told the attorney the truth about everything that happened and that they were trying to make me look like the bad guy. He tried to find out if there had been any bad blood between us previously, and I told him no, other than Paul not liking me and shooting down all of my ideas.

He told me that he appreciated my honesty because he already heard the violent message that I left on Paul's voice mail, which was inadmissible in the state of Michigan. He also told me that I would be served with the restraining order, which would attempt to prevent me from purchasing a weapon, but they were too late, because I already had done that. That was Paul's way of trying to keep me down since I didn't work for them any longer, and trying to cut me off at the knees, like I couldn't stand alone in this and didn't have anyone to support me or hold me up. I was standing by myself, whereas I used to find myself standing with Slim, but, oh well, some things never change—same shit, different flies.

On January 4, 2000,my attorney called me into his office and introduced me to his partner, a young black guy. He had to be on the up-andup because he was a black man in partnership with a Jew. I felt comfortable with him and preferred him to represent me in this case and to just use the other attorney for entertainment-related business. He told me that I would be meeting Slim's attorney but to watch out because he could be an arrogant asshole and would definitely try to get my goat.The whole purpose of this was to meet him and to be served with the papers, in order to avoid some strange person I didn't know coming to my home.We met at a restaurant, and I could tell as soon as we walked in that Slim's attorney had been talking to everyone at the bar. I was the only black male there—and the biggest person in the restaurant. As we approached the bar, everyone started whispering. I could tell by the cold looks and the snickering that everyone knew, and I said to myself, "He ain't shit." I already didn't care for him, but he put the icing on the cake. He was just an attorney trying to be big time, but he was sharp. I didn't let him get to me, though, and that pissed him off. I probably pissed him off more than he did me. He tried to serve me right there in front of everyone. I told him that we needed to go in the back and sit down so that I could read the papers first. My attorney said, "Yeah, man, I told you we didn't want to do this so impersonally." We went to the back and sat down, and the guy proved he was an asshole right off the bat. He made it known that he was serving me in this manner as a favor to his friend,my attorney, and that he normally didn't do this. I thought to myself, You're not doing this as a favor, you are doing this because this is the way it's set up. But I didn't say anything to him at that point because I knew he was just trying to test my temper and get me angry.

Slim's attorney kept babbling about how he was doing this as a favor, and he was waiting on me to say something. I just looked at him with this cold blank stare, and he presented me with the papers. He told me how he was going to have me served by a process server, one supposedly bigger than me, which I doubted, but even so it didn't matter because I don't care about size. If the guy had business to take care of, fine—he had business to take care of—it didn't affect me one bit. He said that to see if it would piss me off, and I just said, "Anyway, man, you got something for me to read?" He presented me with a warning of the personal protection order that I would get, which alleged that I threatened to kill Slim and his wife and kid. I said, "Well, that's what he says, but before I sign anything I have to read it." As I was reading it, the lawyer was talking to me steadily, and said, "Well, can you stop reading for a minute. I'm trying to finish talking to you." I said, "Look, man, I'm on my way to work, and I have things to do today. I'm going to read this! And when I finish, if it's to my liking, and when my attorney sees this, I'm going to sign it. I can do two things at once, so you can keep talking." He said, "That's kind of rude for you to read while I'm talking to you," and I said, "Look, man, I don't have anything to say to you, you need to talk to my attorney. I have nothing to say to you."

By this time, he was mad and turning red, and my attorney said, "Yeah, that would be the best way to handle this. He doesn't want anything to do with you, so you can talk to me and I will talk to him." I continued reading, and I said, "Man, some of this looks like chicken scratch. I know you don't expect me to be able to read this. You are going to have to rewrite this." So, he rewrote some things to make them more legible, explaining that he wrote it in line at the grocery store. I finished, shook Slim's attorney's hand, and apologized for not having been able to meet him under better circumstances and left, knowing that I confused the attorney good—because I was nothing like the monster that they portrayed me to be—and that put a smile on my face. I knew that he knew he was going to have a problem on his hands.

On the drive home from work, I was thinking about signing those papers. Even though it was only a warning and not a felony or a misdemeanor, it was my first time ever being in trouble with the law. My dad always said to keep my name clean. I had tainted my family name and embarrassed them for bringing a blemish to my clean name. I had worked hard all my life and had been cheated. Everything was fine until I hooked up with Slim, then things started going downhill. My man is bad luck! I felt like it was time for me to make some personal changes, and I knew when my group, the Wadsquad, blew up and Big Willz Records got on the map, I was going to handle business a lot differently than they had. It seemed like the game was set up for people to get screwed out of money.

I knew that it was possible for everyone to be in accord and that personal protection orders wouldn't be necessary if people wouldn't lie about one another. I couldn't believe he said I threatened his family. He and I started as friends, but now we were enemies. None of that mattered, though, because we were on opposite sides—his side, my side, the black side, the white side.We used to be on the same team, and I blame the division on Paul. I also hold Slim accountable for not being a big enough or mature enough man to see Paul's angle. Hopefully, one day he will wake up, and when he does, Paul is going to catch it. That is if Slim stays sober enough to see it. That's why Paul keeps him fucked up on Ecstasy and Vicodin, which he does through Mark, making Mark the road manager and the supplier. It's too wild for me. I don't need it.

8

THE BIG PAYBACK!

I'm back in the real world. Man, I tell you it's rough. I had gotten caught in the hype when the whole time I was trying to avoid that trap. That's the power of the music game. It was good to be back to work, back to my family and friends, my wife and my children. You can't put a value on that. That's something that you can't relive and have to take for what it's worth. The hardest part about coming back home was dealing with all the questions about what it was like being on the road. I was also dealing with this hatred I felt for Paul and Slim, and I had to check myself because I almost got to the point where it was becoming a racial issue on my part, because I was beginning to look at Jews and white people differently.This wasn't the first time I had been done wrong by whites lying to cover up something else. But then I said to myself,Well, this is life, and people are going to try to screw you over no matter what color they are, especially in this music game.They took it to that level, and I figured I had to be a bigger person than them, rather than fall into the little traps that they were laying for me.

Being back at work was cool, but unfortunately when I got back, I wasn't able to get the position that I was up for and had to work on the line. In fact, I got demoted, and part of the reason for that was jealousy. People who worked with me saw me on television while I was off and were jealous. I was put in the lowest position at the plant, and it was humiliating. I've often wished that things had worked out between Slim and me so I wouldn't have to deal with that humiliation. But that was a pride factor, and pride can get in the way of dignity. My dignity had been affected because I went from being a platinum-selling artist's bodyguard to a person who threw coil springs into boxes. People would walk by and laugh and joke, but it was OK because I knew I had a wife and kids to support.

The supervisors would treat me like shit, and the one who did it the most was a Jewish guy. I tried to look past that, but every time I heard the word "Jewish," it would bother me. Finally, I decided to grow up and see past that, and I kept telling myself not to let the actions of one man deter me. Anyway, they had me doing the shittiest job in the plant one day, and I was listening to the radio, and lo and behold who comes on but Dr. Dre and Slim, on one of my favorite tracks from the "Dr. Dre 2001" album, "Forgot About Dre." One of my coworkers tried to push my buttons, but I didn't let him. I was a little envious at that moment, but I decided to not waste my energy being bitter. I said to myself, OK, I am an average Joe again and that's cool. I've just got to adjust. It seemed like that DJ was rubbing that song in my face because he just kept playing it over and over in a mix. It reminded me of all the shit I had been through with them, the good times and the bad.

I even took a month and a half off from working on this book because I went through a transition. I decided to do something about it, so I got with one of my artists, Acapella, and she and I talked about doing a song called "Shady Bizzness." I wanted her to put my thoughts in a song. I got with Mike, from the Beat Pushers, and he hooked up the beat. Coincidentally, the beat he hooked up was one that I presented to Slim for his new album. Slim liked it, but he wasn't feeling it. I used the song as therapy to get this off my chest since, due to the restraining order, I had no way of communicating my feelings to him. I couldn't mail him anything or speak to him. It hurt me because we had been friends at one time, but Paul sealed that fate, and Slim fed into it, so he was just as guilty. I dealt with all this and used my music as therapy in dealing with the fact that I had no money because Paul and Slim had revoked my pay.

When they did that it put all my business plans on hold. You may ask what can you do with $6,000, but the way I had everything budgeted out, there was plenty I could have done. With the plans put on hold, though, it did give me a chance to finish the song "Shady Bizzness," and the book, which will hopefully lead into a screenplay one day. This is how I got through my feelings, and it felt good; it felt like I was making some progress. I was dealing with the financial problems because I had drained my mutual funds and my savings, and we were still behind. It got to a point where we almost had to file bankruptcy because of the money that we were owed from Paul and Slim.We had already written checks against that money, and that put me in a position where I had to work overtime, which my employers weren't offering a lot of.

My wife was also under a lot of stress. In the turn of a day, I went from being comfortable to damn near poverty level—and I had taken care of these guys! I talked to my attorney, Barton Morris, Jr., a young brother about thirty-two years of age, and convinced him to take on my case at 33 percent commission. Mike had said he would represent me for free, but I couldn't even get a return call from him. I think, with him being friends with Paul's lawyer, they somehow had convinced him not to even deal with me. I don't want to get into why I suspect that, but I think it has to do with them both being Jewish and not really wanting to step on each other's toes. I can understand that, but I just wish he had told me the deal instead of just cutting me off the way he did. Anyway, Mike decided to allow Barton to take on my case, and he is a great man for that because he didn't have to do that. Barton has been doing good work, and it has made me feel like some progress was being made, but at the same time I realized that getting the money owed me was going to be a long, drawn-out process. I was OK with that as long as I could sue to get my money back.

I had to deal with the repercussions of resigning from working with Slim. I did have the urge to call him to see if we could make things right, but I would look at my kids and think of the way he treated me in the past and realize that I would be a fool to go back for more of the same ill treatment. They screwed me over once, so they would do it again. Dignity, pride, and prayer helped me through that. God really guided me toward the right path on this decision, and in dealing with this rebound situation and trying to get the bills paid. By this time, Slim had won a Grammy, so a considerable amount of time had passed. I had forgiven him, but I hadn't forgotten. I wanted to show them that you don't do good people bad.You don't do anyone bad, for that matter. I guess I had to act a fool on this guy to finally get some respect. Money isn't everything, and true wealth is family. My father always taught me that. He told me that you can go all around the world, but if you don't have your family with you then everything is worthless. I really had learned and believed that at this point.

I spent my time in the studio working on the song "Shady Bizzness" and thinking about getting my label back together because people in my group had stopped calling. I guess that since I quit working for Slim, they felt as if I had blown their chances for success. In all actuality, there was no opportunity there. You have to create your own opportunities. Unfortunately, we had a couple of weak links there. I had now weeded out who was real and who was fake among my crew – or I should say they weeded themselves out. I expected more of them to be around, especially during this time, when their support was really needed, but unfortunately they left and went looking for another bandwagon to jump on. I kept myself busy keeping contact with the connections I had made on the road and keeping in touch with the remaining true members of the Wadsquad.

We held meetings and talked about how the situation with Slim affected us, and they understood that we were in the same position we were in before we met them, and that we just had to keep moving forward. I could see the bitterness of the Wadsquad toward Slim, but I told them that was my beef and they shouldn't worry about it. But they saw it as a family affair type of thing, like by Slim messing with me he was messing with them, and they took it personally.They were basically supportive, and I decided to use Slim as my motivation for success in the music business. It was negative that he had done me wrong, but there was no better way to get revenge than with my own success.

A lot of things were now in the open, but Slim had fabricated a lot of lies. That boy was not born in Detroit, so he is not from Detroit. He is always hollering trailer park, but there are no trailer parks in Detroit. He is from a trailer park in Marine City, about twenty-eight miles into the country. Even his own crew members questioned his honesty about where he was from. He had skills anyway, so why did he lie? He may have lived in Detroit a couple of months, and he may have even worked in Detroit, but he is not from Detroit. Now I see why his own mother stepped forward the way that she did regarding a lot of the things that he did and said. I don't really know a lot about his relationship with his mother, but I am sure that there is truth in both of their stories. He has everyone thinking that he came up in Detroit a little white boy and fought his way to platinum status, but that's not the truth. He has skills, no one can take that from him, but the important thing is to be true to yourself and to your fans, but it's a little too late for that now. That's the same thing that Vanilla Ice did. Slim, you contradicted yourself.You grew up in a trailer park like you said, but there are no trailer parks in Detroit.

When I first started writing this book, it was out of revenge. My father always told me that if you dig one hole for someone to fall in, you may as well dig two because you are going to need one of them for yourself. I always kept that in mind as I was writing this book. At the same time, the book of Proverbs tells us that there is a time to fight and a time

Big-Naz and bodyguards introduce "Shady Bizzness" to Detroit metro Borders book signing.

to walk away. I walked away so I could fight, because I was in a no-win situation. I wasn't fighting physically; I was hitting them in their pockets and in their fan base with the truth. I was telling it the way it happened. This is nothing personal, Paul and Slim. This is the real deal.

Now that I have closure and am using Slim as my motivation for success, I finally put my plaques on the wall. They remind me of everything I went through, and one day they are going to be worth some money because he is going to do something stupid like OD, and I am going to have to lock them up in a vault to keep them from being stolen. I do wish them both the best though, and I pray for them often. I pray for them to change their ways, because there are a lot of people out there whom they owe money to and a lot of folks out there whom they disrespected. There are a lot of folks out there who want to hurt them. They may not know it, but there are quite a few people out there, on both coasts, who want to do something to these guys. I hope and pray for their safety because they are going to need it.

I did the song and the book. People have called me crazy for doing these things, but that's OK because I am crazy. To make it in the music business you have to have a gimmick or you have to have talent, one or the other. It just so happens we have both in my crew. I decided to put the song "Shady Bizzness" out on the Wadsquad EP to let the world know how Slim is. This is also my way of talking to him since I can't talk to him personally, due to the restraining order, so I plan to use mass communication to get my points across. My attorney and I have gotten together to try to get Paul and Slim to come to court, and, not surprisingly, they have canceled every time. Paul and Slim didn't expect me to fight for my money, so of course they were intimidated. Rather than face me like men they chose to flee, like they usually do. They had hoped for my money to run out, so that I would no longer be able to afford my attorney. By the blessing of God, however, my attorney agreed to take my case on a contingency basis, so I have nothing but time. In fact, my attorney charged more than theirs, but I was able to negotiate a feasible deal, and Paul and Slim couldn't understand that. They realized that they weren't the only ones with some connections and some pull. They were obviously nervous, and I loved it.

The whole month of February, Paul and Slim kept canceling court dates. Finally, the judge subpoenaed them to come to court. At this point, Slim and Paul talked to their attorney to try to cut a deal to drop the gun provision, so that I could keep my gun permits, but to keep the restraining order in effect until they got their personal items back. I told them no deal. I wanted my money. My attorney made a bold move by calling for a hearing, but Slim knew that if he showed up, the tables could turn on him for brandishing a weapon, and he could be prosecuted for a firearm felony. Paul, Slim and their attorney knew this and knew that they were the odd men out now. They knew they had fucked up when they lied and said I threatened their families. I never threatened to kill anybody.

March 15, 2000

I was on the Internet checking my e-mail and, much to my surprise, I got a return e-mail from XXL magazine.They wrote that they were interested in hearing more of my story on Eminem. I got in touch with the assistant editor,Vanessa Satten. She told me they were interested in doing an exclusive interview about this book, which I agreed to do in exchange for a contact to help me publish this book, a close-up story on this book, and an article on the Wadsquad with pictures. She said she would present that to her boss. I told her that Slim and his manager, Paul, hate this magazine with a passion and that they denounce XXL worldwide everywhere they go and that Slim even makes a remark in his raps about using XXL as toilet paper. I told her to tell her boss this information as well. Later, she called me back and told me that they agreed to negotiate what we discussed and to have my lawyer take care of the legal end of the deal.We agreed as well, and we're going to be doing the story.The plan was to drop it during Slim's second album release.

On March 22nd, Paul and Slim canceled another court date, so we decided to play some hardball. I had my lawyer subpoena Kim, Slim's wife, to be one of my witnesses. It would work out perfectly because there was rumor of divorce in early March. She would have no problem taking my side because, allegedly, she was trying to take him for all he had anyway. When Paul and Slim saw Kim's name right next to one of his mistresses' name on the witness list, they freaked out, their attorney freaked out, and they didn't know what to do. Immediately, they wanted to make a deal and pay the money back that they owed me.They knew that we would get Kim to open up, and when we were finished providing her with certain information, she would take him for even more money. They wanted to play hardball, so we brought out the aluminum bats! And we didn't strike out! So, Slim and Paul went back to the dugout.

On March 29th, Slim and Paul reneged once again on coming to court, which was to be expected.They did agree to pay me $4,300, which was my Christmas bonus and a week's pay, but actually they owed me more than that. By this time it was more than the money, though. It was about dignity and self-worth and showing them that they weren't the only ones who knew people in high places.They may have had big money, but you don't always have to have big money to fight battles. It is ironic that the name of Paul's company is Goliath Artists, but we all know what happened to Goliath—David killed him with a slingshot. I felt like I just killed Goliath. I felt like I had a new lease on life, and I learned a lot from working with these guys. I learned a lot in a positive manner but I learned even more in a negative manner. On a positive note, Shady Tours taught me to stay busy and to use my connections. That's how you keep your name out there and never rest. On a negative note, Slim and Paul didn't take care of their people. When the Wadsquad arrives, they will be well cared for. You shouldn't cut yourself short in taking care of people, but those guys were just greedy. I learned how to be driven and to have motivation. It's always been business, but Paul and Slim made it personal. I am keeping it business.

News Flash!

I knew it would only be a matter of time before Eminem would influence Slim Shady to get Marshall Mathers in trouble. It's amazing to be on the other side of the fence watching Slim self-destruct. I've always known that Kim would be the downfall of his career. Slim had seen all the signs but refused to acknowledge them. Slim once told me about a dream he had. The dream involved him being arrested in a public place for an unknown reason, while Kim pranced around in a very, very short skirt that showed her panties. During that time, Slim had suspected Kim of cheating. Slim actually had a premonition of his fate. As we all know, Slim was arrested for pistol-whipping a guy for kissing his wife in the parking lot of a nightclub.

Slim was given a tip that his wife was cheating on him, and he should see for himself. Lo and behold, he came, he saw, and he whipped some ass. Unfortunately, his jealous rage earned him a felonious assault charge and and another charge for brandishing a firearm. Both are punishable up to nine years. Twelve hours prior to that event, Slim had pulled his gun and threatened to shoot a member of ICP at a car audio shop.

A few days later, he was arraigned on both gun charges for two separate events. My questions were:Why are you still brandishing a weapon? Why are you carrying an empty gun? How many more people will you brandish your weapon in front of before you're shot? The news of his downfall was a disappointing event. It was obvious that he had no one in his corner to consult him or control him. That's what I did best for Slim. I kept him out of trouble constantly. I felt some guilt seeing him in handcuffs. I should have been there. Slim made the statement that he carries a gun due to the absence of his bodyguard! I thought I'd be glad to see him fall, but all I could think about was how he was blowing it. After all the bullshit and misery he put me through, I was concerned about his future. At the rate he's going, he's headed for jail or the morgue. Think, Slim! Your life should be lived for Hailey's benefit.The media has labeled him a "joker," a "Tupac wanna be," and a "lyrical tough guy."

Well, Kim has finally earned the limelight she wanted, but through a mug shot. Apparently, Kim and Slim were tussling that night in the parking lot. When the police came to arrest Marshall, she attacked the cops. She was booked on disorderly conduct.The next day, Kim released a statement to the media about staying out of their private life. She also made a public plea that she stands by her man. RIGHT! Slim always said, "There's no such thing as bad press." Slim Shady is the talk of the town across the world. He is bigger than Elvis right now. Many people wonder, Will he last? Will he be another rapper dead for popping off at the mouth for something he shouldn't have said? Will he OD like Elvis? I think neither. I believe he's going to kill Kim for REAL, or she going to kill him during one of their nasty spells. Then again, God may intervene and call Slim to be a preacher! Now that would be a sight to see! (Minister Marshall Mathers, aka Triple "M"). I worry about Kim and Slim and hope their marriage doesn't end in tragedy. Hailey needs them both to be mature parents.

Financially, Slim has possibly dug himself a hole. The guy that he pistol-whipped is suing Slim for an undisclosed amount. The victim said he feared for his life as Slim threatened to kill him. I estimate the victim will sue for $25 million. PAY UP!!! It's a sad day when a guy takes your wife and your money. Well, that definitely puts his mom at the back of the lawsuit line. It's probably a good thing I did resign, because I wouldn't have gotten another raise. I guess you really do reap what you sow!

Slim got away with flashing his gun during OUR confrontation because the police were acting like fans instead of cops. Think of how he shortchanged his staff for security, producers, and arrangements. We're talking thousands of dollars people haven't been paid, especially in production. God doesn't like ugly, because you'll pay, one way or another! It's weird to see Slim's songs come to life in a timely manner, especially the song "Kim." This is the track where he raps about killing her for cheating. Then there's the song "Criminal," where he likens his words to criminal behavior. Unfortunately, his actions spoke louder than his words when he earned two felony firearm assault charges. Congratulations!

Marshall Mathers had put himself in an uncompromising position (no pun intended) with the homosexual community. Slim went out of his way to bash the gay and lesbian community through violent expressions. Michigan gay activists fired back, trying to have his music pulled from the shelves. They felt that Slim was encouraging teens to batter and possibly murder gays and lesbians. These gay activists wanted Slim to feel their pain.

This is an official announcement that Slim Shady has won the beef with XXL. On June 20, 2000, XXL nervously dropped my exclusive interview about Slim. They'd been shaken down! XXL said, "We think Slim Shady and his entourage may rush our office with trouble. This concerns our employees!" I wrote it off as a unique situation because XXL started the beef by calling Slim a "culture stealer." Slim retaliated by dissing the magazine globally. I worked diligently for six months on this exclusive with XXL, and they bailed a week before the release. I took it as a minor setback and realized that this was huge to XXL. Obviously, they couldn't handle a history-making story of this magnitude. I must say, I was disappointed when XXL dropped my story, especially after doing leads ("Remember, we got a big bodyguard!"). Blacks don't get many chances to stand together against a white powerhouse without someone selling out. Next time, stick to your guns! Slim does!

Lastly, Slim's fans have put him as their savior. A god? He has cult followers that threatened the prosecuting attorney with death threats if he was prosecuted for his gun charges. The prosecutor took the threats seriously and moved his family to safety. Utterly amazing! They can hurt Slim more than they can help. As time goes on and his career continues to grow, I'll be looking forward to the shocking news he hasn't made yet.This is just the beginning!

Stop the Presses!

Kim attempted suicide on July 7, 2000, at 11:30 pm., after allegedly confronting Slim Shady about my book, "Shady Bizzness." When Kim confronted Slim at his concert in Auburn Hills, he apparently didn't deny the claims. She then rushed home and attempted suicide by slashing her wrist with five superficial wounds. Slim Shady's mother was quoted in a tabloid as saying, "Kim planned the suicide attempt for attention. Nobody attempts suicide in front of their family."

Rumor has it that Momma Mathers is writing a song about her son, Marshall. Hmmm...! I wonder where she got that idea.

More News

Finally, the dreaded question! Did Slim sleep with Christina Aguilera? No! Absolutely not! The one time he tried to approach Christina she shut him down. That happened at the MTV Europe Awards in 1999. However, Christina thought he was cute. Slim apparently had crushes on Christina and Britney Spears. Obviously Slim's feelings were hurt when the ladies didn't respond. Therefore, he lashed out at them in "The Real Slim Shady" video.

As far as N'SYNC and The Backstreet Boys—he had plenty of opportunities to fight them.We often stayed in the same hotels with them when they were in New York, LA, and sometimes Europe. Slim never made any complaints to me about N'SYNC or The Backstreet Boys. How can one scrawny MC kick five or more guy's asses at once? Draw your own conclusion on the "Real Slim Shady."

Detroit Free Press

SATURDAY June 10, 2000

Page 3A

SECOND FRONT PAGE

WWW.FREEP.COM

Target of Eminem's rage sues

He says altercation scared him

By M.L. Elrick
Free Press Staff Writer

The man who received the kiss that put Eminem on front pages of newspapers for something other than selling millions of records sued the rapper Friday, claiming that he still fears for his life five days after the alleged attack.

"I never wanted to live so bad in my life until those few minutes," said John Guerra, 26, of Warren. Outside the courthouse, he recounted his struggle with Eminem over the gun the apparently jealous entertainer pointed at him early Sunday outside Hot Rocks Cafe in Warren.

"I still shake about it," Guerra said. "It was the scariest moment of my life."

Guerra's lawsuit, which seeks an unspecified amount in damages and was filed in Macomb County Circuit Court, accuses Eminem of hitting Guerra in the head and face. Guerra is also seeking damages for emotional distress. He said Eminem twice told him, "I'm going to kill you" as they struggled for control of the unloaded gun.

Eminem, whose real name is Marshall Mathers III and who is also known as Slim Shady, was arraigned Wednesday on felony charges of assault and carrying a concealed weapon after police and prosecutors said he saw his wife kissing Guerra and erupted in a jealous rage.

Although Macomb County Prosecutor Carl Marlinga said Guerra told police he received "a rather intimate kiss" from Eminem's wife, Kimberly Mathers, Guerra told reporters "it was just a simple, friendly kiss."

Mathers told the Free Press on Tuesday that she gave him and several friends a hug and peck on the cheek before parting after a Saturday night out.

John Guerra

On Thursday, Eminem was arraigned in Royal Oak on a felony charge of carrying a concealed weapon and a misdemeanor charge of brandishing a firearm in public. Police and Oakland County prosecutors accused him of flashing his weapon during a spat with an associate of rival Detroit-area rap act Insane Clown Posse.

Eminem's attorney, Howard Hertz, said Friday that the rapper would be cleared of the charges. Hertz declined comment on Guerra's lawsuit.

Eminem posted bond on both the Macomb and Oakland county charges and will begin a two-month tour June 16 in San Diego.

➤ *See the Free Press profile on Eminem at* **www.freep.com/fun/music/qemin28.htm**

Contact **M.L. ELRICK** *at 810-469-8087 or elrick@freepress.com.*

9

THE AFTERMATH

People often ask me, "What happened after the book went public?" Plenty! The behind-the-scene drama was better than the book.The media went crazy with this "tell all" by lifting up then tearing down a "disgruntled employee." If I was disgruntled, I would have went out like a US Postal worker! There were media scams and attempted bootlegging by a certain weekly entertainment magazine. This particular magazine was scheduled to do a review and allegedly`sold copies to Eminem and Paul. There's no doubt in my mind that they leaked the material, because absolutely no one else had the draft. I received further confirmation from two New York sources that were outside the Eminem camp that had copies of the partial book. One was a law student, and the other was DT. They read aloud to me my material verbatim.

Needless to say, I was pissed! I was pissed at my publicist and this jackass journalist. In addition to this, I was receiving threatening calls from the media saying, "This book better be the real deal and come out on time! Or we're going to eat your ass alive!" I told this journalist, "The media will be kissing my ass and savoring the sweet taste, so pucker up!"

I experienced many games with the media like jockeying for position against Eminem in a magazine. Reporters would do exclusive interviews and set publishing dates on the stories only to have material to obtain an interview with Eminem. Eminem would agree to take the inter views and that would shut down my story.The magazines never had intentions of going with my stories. I was just a pawn. However, for every story that didn't flourish, another one did. I eventually did over 500 interviews domestic and abroad via the Internet, magazines, radio, and TV.The media probably hated me more than his fans for publishing the book. Why? Eminem was the second coming of Elvis. The Great White Hope! The Golden Boy! Therefore nothing should be said to tarnish his image, true or false. There were so many double standards for Eminem. All of a sudden, white people who hated hip-hop were professional music critics on Eminem and the industry. Please! He could do no wrong. I searched high and low for book deals only to learn that I was being blackballed. I never met so many scared professionals in my life. "Oh, you have a great book, but Marshall might sue us! However, if he dies tragically we'll publish it," said publishers.

Three months before the book dropped I did a worldwide media blitz that caused Paul and Slim to pitch an insulting $25,000 offer to buy me out. Needless to say, I turned them down and offered them several opportunities at a fair wage: $1,000,000, negotiable. That fee would compensate me for the worldwide book publishing rights, merchandising, and film/ video rights. I was willing to negotiate down from my offer, but they were stuck on $25,000. No deal. Shortly afterward I published the book independently and sold 1,000 books the first week through self-distribution. Unfortunately, the demand was so great that it was difficult to keep up with sales. If I had a publisher, I would have sold at least 100,000 books that first week. I was getting calls for books worldwide. I handled the demand fairly well considering the financial circumstances. My wife, mom and dad, and brother took loans from their 401Ks to help fund the printing and publicity. I was cashing checks left and right to pay my attorney, Stephanie Hammonds, my CPA, Kevin Carter, my publicist, Roger Neal, Onyx Printing, and my assistant, Adam Rogers. I had people on payroll for eighteen months after the publishing date. I must say, the book did well for an independent. It did so well that EMINEM released a songbook titled "Angry Blond" a few months after mine. Needless to say, fans were disappointed. They were expecting a rebuttal to my book or a novel. I believe it was published to knock the edge off my book sales, considering "Shady Bizzness" was the first book EVER published about him. I eventually sold 10,000 books independently with no publisher and limited distribution.

I must admit everything wasn't peachy. There were times when I wished I had never written the book or ever met Eminem. My life had become consumed with a one-time friend turned enemy. The book took on a life of its own, causing emotional trauma. I started to hate the book as much as I did Eminem. In reality, I hated myself. Why did I write the book? The book was an outlet to channel my anger and to prevent myself from possibly serving life in prison. The book was therapy for my thoughts instead of penal corrections for my possible actions. Several situations occurred that made me bitter toward the book. The first was the failed movie offers from some major film houses. These film producers would make great offers but they couldn't deliver the royalties or a fair contract. In other words, their mouths were writing checks their asses couldn't sign. Then there was one particular UK publisher whom my attorney negotiated with for eight months to land a worldwide publishing deal. The deal entailed publishing "Shady Bizzness" three months before the release of "8 Mile," with a media blitz. Everything was great until three weeks before the release date when the publisher pulled out of the deal. I was blown away. This publisher made me jump through so many hoops that I felt like a dog in the circus. I changed the title of the book. I added pictures. I deleted material per their attorney, and they still dropped me! The publisher claimed they were nervous about the controversial content. However, I did manage to get 50 percent of the signing bonus. I was devastated. That was a multimillion dollar deal to coincide with the release of "8 Mile". I allowed the book to go downhill for one year. I didn't promote it or publish another single copy. I said, "I quit! Fuck this book and fuck Eminem!" It got so bad that my kids would be scared to chant Eminem songs from the radio. This book toyed with my emotions and often rekindled the day I left Marshall with guns drawn. Eminem added fuel to the fire by lying in Blender magazine two years after the book was published. Blender magazine released this quote from Eminem. "I came to find out that he was keeping a fucking journal! That was his plan ever since he met me. I was his shot at fame. After that happened, I didn't trust anybody."What the hell was he talking about? As I recall, they sought me out for the job and I originally turned them down. As God is my witness I never kept a journal. If I wanted fame, I would've went out like John Wilkes Booth. Now, there's your shot at fame. Blender magazine should be careful whom they call an unethical bodyguard, especially after not asking for my side of the story.

After a year hiatus from "Shady Bizzness," I received a call from the Jenny Jones Show for an in-studio interview. This was just the spark I needed to bounce back from my layoff. Little did I know there would be a series of events to follow. Upon arriving in Chicago for the taping of the Jenny Jones Show, I received a mystery call. The call was regarding someone seeking publishing for another Eminem exposé. I immediately thought that it was a setup for shady dealings. This call came one hour before taping the Jenny Jones Show. I knew Jenny was going to hit me from every angle possible, and she did. Little did I know, the show was set up for me to be the antagonist. This show included Eminem lookalikes, former coworkers, and his grandma. Before I could sit down, there were boos and negative remarks from his granny. I kept my composure and remained standing, posing for the haters in a cream white suit, matching head to toe. I was killing them softly! When the crowd settled down, I then sat down. Immediately, Granny stated, "You wanted to harm my grandson!" And I honestly replied, "Yes, it wasn't the right thing to do, but that's how I felt. So instead of hurting him, I wrote the book!" Then out of nowhere, Jenny Jones hits me with the Eminem quote from Blender, which was great. This allowed me to address the lies and make people understand I never had intentions of writing the book until Slim and Paul revoked my funds, and the conflict that took place outside his mother-in law's home happened. Eventually I won the crowd over, but you'd never know that by the way they edited the interview. Eminem's grandma was a good sport because we conversed during the commercial breaks about how she missed her grandson. She even pitched a proposal for me to help her publish her book. I had considered helping her just because of her struggling financial situation. I could never understand how Eminem could allow his mom and granny to go without while he lives high on the hog. It must be a cultural thing. Regardless of whatever happened in the past, family should live in comfort.

10

BEHIND THE SCENES

Two days after the Jenny Jones Show I got another mystery call regarding someone publishing an Eminem book. This particular fellow called with plenty of anxiety and desperation in his voice, which made me nervous. Reluctantly I agreed to meet with this guy, but I told him, "This better not be a setup for a HIT! If so, I'll shoot you on sight. I'm talking self-defense." He agreed to be strictly about business.We both agreed to meet in Eastpointe, Michigan, at the Big Boy restaurant. I must say there were times when this book made me extremely paranoid, and I was my own bodyguard. There have been times when crazed Eminem fans have noticed me and rushed me to ask questions but their body language spoke differently, which caused them to get a rude awakening. One particular time at the gas station, this guy was pumping gas and noticed me. He kept aggressively questioning if I was Eminem's ex-bodyguard. After the second firm yes, he reached into his car. I then reached into my waistband and grabbed my gun. The guy turned around abruptly and walked toward me in a fast-paced manner. Immediately he stopped in his tracks upon observing the cold piece of steel.Then he says, "Dude I just wanted you to sign my book. I read your book in one night. It's the best book I ever read!" I holstered my firearm, and then graciously apologized and explained my response to his fanatical behavior.

Now that I agreed to meet this mystery caller about this new Eminem book, I prepared for the worst. Once again I put on the bulletproof vest, got my extra clip, loaded the firearm. I contacted backup to stand by in the event something happened. Some may call it crazy, but I believe in facing my demons instead of running from them. Upon pulling up in the parking lot, I cased the area for anything unusual or out of place before entering. The mystery man and I agreed to meet in front of the restaurant. I had taken my firearm and placed it in a small handbag in which my hand could fire the weapon without exposing the gun. Shortly afterwards, as I stood there, a Puerto Rican/Caucasian male approaches me–the mystery caller.We entered the building and took a booth in the rear. I sat where I could see the door and placed my small handbag on the table pointed right at his chest. Observing the mystery man's body language and the way he constantly adjusted, he was armed also. After the first five minutes we both began to realize it was strictly business. He pitched to me that his wife was a former friend of Kim Mathers and volunteer nanny for Hailey. He also suspected that Eminem had slept with his wife. He and his wife were in the process of filing for divorce due to differences and possible infidelity. He wanted to publish an exposé about Eminem and Kim as payback for what had transpired. The only problem was bringing his soon-to-be ex-wife on board. He pitched the whole idea about me publishing the book, and needless to say after reading the draft, I wasn't going to risk that. I read that draft several times and contacted the husband with a counterproposal. I basically proposed to them that I would be their publicist and distributor of the book. The major problem was that no one could know I was involved with their book or it would never take off. Therefore, I took on a Jewish alias, "Silas Bernstein," CEO of Urban Tabloid Marketing and Distribution. Man, it worked like a charm! I then realized how powerful the Jewish community is in the entertainment and media.

The mystery man convinced his wife they should remain together and publish this book. She agreed, and we set a deadline for release of the book, "Cleaning Out My Closet" by J.R.Watkins. I, Silas Bernstein, masterminded a plan for the husband to drop the book on Eminem's 30th birthday, October 17, 2002.The media blitz went off like the Fourth of July. I sent out press releases worldwide under my alias Silas Bernstein and the media ate it up! The media is biased, and I proved that through the media campaign. The media is so quick to believe a Caucasian author's story faster than a black author's story. The same media that accepted and embraced J.R Watkins' book, rejected my book. On October 30, 2002, Q955's Mojo awakened Eminem on his 30th birthday in the morning (Detroit, MI). J.R.Watkins exclusively released her story along with shame- less plugs for sales. I sat back and just watched my media blitz unravel with perfection. My new identity as Mr. Bernstein blazed a trail from Los Angeles to the UK. Everyone was requesting interviews from Silas Bernstein's client, J.R. Watkins. I laughed my ass off! The media never knew until now. Surprise!!! The same biased media that wouldn't give me any reviews were paying us to get J.R.Watkins' story. And her story didn't come cheap. Her book debuted on Amazon.com at #152 out of one million books. In a matter of two months since meeting, I had showed J.R.Watkins how to self-publish and promote her own book. My former experience of self-publishing didn't come cheap, and therefore I got paid. Unfortunately, the more money they made, the more they wanted to do my job and take control of distribution. I'm a businessman, and our contract had to be honored. We eventually went our separate ways in agreeing to disagree after selling about 1,400 books in a matter of eight months. It was a unique experience and I'm glad I was able to assist them. However, as business goes, we pulled the book from distributors and media, never to be seen again.There were bitter times, but the mystery man and I shook hands and embraced in a hug after I gave them their last royalty check.We agreed that we should try again in the future. Needless to say, Kim Mathers wasn't too happy about the book being published from her ex-best friend. The book highlighted Kim's drug problems, spending sprees, and Eminem's love life with Mariah Carey and many other inside stories.

11

NEW NEWS

I hate to say I told you so, but I told you so! I knew there would be other shocking news from the hip-hop Bonnie and Clyde. Kim has managed to catch several cases concerning drunk driving to drug possession. She's been caught with cocaine twice in the amounts close to a kilo and she's still on the streets? Crack peddlers in the hood get two to five years for a rock of cocaine for possession and intent to distribute. Like I've always said, long money never goes to jail. Kim has posted bail at $50,000 on two known occasions only to never report back to court. She then turns fugitive and throws hotel drug parties only to be raided in her absence. Also she's thrown her sister from a moving limo, butt-ass naked. Now that's gangster! She's more hardcore and gangster than 95 percent of the rappers in the industry. Lately, Kim Mathers can be seen on the news in a mug shot. She has managed to escape twice from treatment facilities while serving her term for drugs. Personally, I think they should just leave her alone, because all they're doing is pissing off taxpayers and making money off her drug problem when she posts bail and released. The judicial system appears to be cashing in on her fame, literally. Kim's radical behavior has cost her to lose custody of Hailey and for the judge to rule in Marshall's favor. Kim has sent Marshall on a roller-coaster ride by having a new baby with another man who wasn't allowed to see the baby. Marshall and Kim had temporarily gotten back together to raise Hailey and his new stepdaughter. Marshall has been making a valid effort to keep Kim sober and out of legal trouble by allowing her to move into his $7 million mansion, purchased from the CEO of Kmart. Folks, I'm not making this up. It's all public information.

Debbie Mathers was carjacked, unbelievably on the now worldfamous 8 Mile Road. A black male teenager attacked her at gunpoint. She was left with bruises and a broken foot. She said she was lucky to be alive because as her attacker's gun jammed as he went to fire. Needless to say, he got away with her vehicle. Debbie Mathers called Eminem with the news, only to be cursed out by her son. Eminem said, "Of all the fucking places for this to happen, you get jacked where I shot my movie?" He didn't believe her and thought this was another publicity stunt on her behalf. In more somber Debbie Mathers news, she has been diagnosed with breast cancer and has sought her son's assistance. Eminem's managers sought medical benefits for his estranged mother only to be denied because of her existing condition. Debbie Mathers then requested financial aid to receive radiation therapy. Debbie Mathers was down to eighty pounds and was always sick because of the lack of proper medical treatment for her cancer. Debbie Mathers said her son had yet to reply to her request for financial assistance for radiation. That is truly fucked up! Marshall, man, let that nonsense go before it's too late!

EMINEM gets a Bad Dick Report? Remember Kessia? She was Eminem's mistress during his early stages of marriage with Kim. Kessia was the one he kicked off the tour in Germany. Well she has spoken, and man, was she loud. She did an exclusive interview with a reputable UK newspaper and said that Eminem was terrible in bed. She claimed that Marshall had problems with premature ejaculation and could only have about one minute of sex. Damn, man! Is there a doctor in the house? If so, please help him and his little friend. No man deserves a BDR (Bad Dick Report). That's worse than bad credit. That blemish stays there for life. I knew that Kessia would someday emerge, and she did it with bells and whistles. Much props to Kessia for giving me kudos on my book and validating everything I spoke about. Thanks, Kessia.

Is EMINEM a racist? How about them money-hungry black bitches! Well, that's what he said! He also referred to black people as niggers and moon crickets. What is a moon cricket? That's like a future racial slur, 2050. No man can measure the racism in a man's heart and obviously he had plenty buried there. Everyone keeps saying that it was in the past. Hell, David Duke, ex- KKK, advocated the killing of blacks and Jews. I'll never forget that. Why should we forget what Eminem said?

The problem really doesn't lie with Eminem; the problem lies with these Uncle Tom record executives and radios DJs excusing Eminem's statements.These Black professionals will say and do anything to kiss Master's ass in order to keep their business ventures or jobs. If Eminem had made an anti-semitic remark, he'd be out of business. His records would've been pulled from shelves and became a mere myth. Plus, he would have been forced to give a public apology.That's the truth! I know it's hard to swallow, so gulp twice.

The Source magazine exposes EMINEM as a racist. Fans, don't hate on The Source! After all, it was a white guy that narced Eminem to the public. Eminem's former Caucasian buddies sold the tape to the magazine because Eminem was misrepresenting himself.These particular guys were once in a rap group with Marshall.The group was truly hurt when Eminem didn't reach back and help them to the next level. These guys felt as if the movie "8 Mile" was a joke. They claimed that during Eminem's underground years, everybody from the producers to the rappers in his crew were white.That caused them to deflate the air from Eminem's fame. It was not the Source magazine that sought out the tape, the tape was brought to them. I commend The Source magazine for their honesty and bravery in journalism. The article written in the February 2004 issue was award-winning. The Source magazine went so far as to release snippets of the songs with the magazine.They did this with proper approval from the courts to ensure no copyright violation. In May 2004, Eminem countersued The Source magazine for infringement, and the case was appealed in NYC ruling in Eminem's favor.The Great White Hope does it again. He's untouchable. The only thing that can stop him is Uncle Sam and the grim reaper. If he can find a loophole on the grim reaper, he'll work that angle to death. No pun intended.

Did you hear about EMINEM versus BENZINO? So who won the battle of the lyrical beef? Lyrically, Eminem was of course was more talented. However, the topics Benzino touched on were serious and for real. It had me thinking Eminem was going to get shot! Allegedly the beef started when 50 Cent was to sign with Benzino's record label but was intercepted by Shady Records. As the ex-bodyguard, I was able to see and hear plenty of things and I know for a fact that in 1999 in Germany, Eminem spoke of signing 50 Cent when he heard him on a dis song about Jay-Z. Realistically, Eminem should leave the beefs alone because the industry is already waiting for him to die. There have been so many rumors of his death and the media always call me to confirm the truth.Why do they rush his death? God forbid something tragic happens to Eminem; so many people stand to make a pretty penny off of his legacy.That includes record companies, fans, merchandisers, bootleggers, and unfortunately, authors. I pray for Eminem, his family and record label every day. EMINEM music used on terrorist prisoners. On May 14, 2004, two British men detained in the US prison camp at Guantanamo Bay, Cuba, alleged they were tortured and forced to listen to Eminem at deafening volume levels. The two men described their abuse in an open letter to George Bush which was released by the New York-based Center for Constitutional Rights.We all know that some of these men at the Cuban prison were sodomized. I'm sure the most requested songs were "Just Don't Give a Fuck" and "Still Don't Give A Fuck!"

What is Byron doing? I still do some occasional bodyguard work. I've had the pleasure of working with Lil' Mo and the WNBA, plus a few Michigan state representatives. I'm currently taking advantage of entrepreneurship, hitting the weights heavy, attending the gun range, enjoying life, and raising my family of five. I've been blessed to have such a supporting cast during this craziness over the last four years. FYI, I don't hate Eminem. Seriously. I've made several attempts to contact Paul Rosenberg directly and made peace treaty offers only to be turned away. Oh well, I tried. I look forward to burying the hatchet because life is too short. Besides, my kids love his songs and always ask questions about him. God has blessed me with opportunities to appear in Eminem documentaries, a few independent films, release new music, and write new books. In conclusion, I'd like to make sure folks know that I'm a Christian with a potty mouth. I believe in God wholeheartedly, but I'm not perfect. In other words, get off my ass about the profanity. I put that language there for the fans. I wanted you to feel the tension and stress. Lastly, I thank you for purchasing and reading this book for the first time or maybe second time around. Keep your eyes open, because "Shady Bizzness" the Movie will be even better.

Recuperating in Hawaii from the dislocated shoulder I got watching out for Slim.

EPILOGUE: PAPER GANGSTER

What is a Paper Gangster? It's a person that uses his or her pen as a weapon to seek the downfall of another individual. There are no boundaries with a Paper Gangster, because the power of the pen allows them to kill you again and again. The victim of a Paper Gangster usually finds him or herself confined to the boundaries of the lines of a notebook or a contract. Who are these Paper Gangsters? Most of them are rappers who talk tough in the studio by dissing others on tracks. Later they wish they could retract their statements, while they hired four bodyguards to watch their backs.Who are the others? They are shady CPAs, shady lawyers, and shady managers in the entertainment field.They claim to have their client's best interest at hand, but the only interest they have is the one they withdraw from their client's accounts in excessive amounts. Paper Gangsters are epidemic.As soon you get rid of one, another spawns more sickness in this industry. No matter how tough they talk and conniving they may seem, their only weapon is a pen and nothing more.

APPENDIX

The following pages show some of the documents sent to me to keep me away from Slim and the checks they gave me that they stopped payment on.

STATE OF MICHIGAN

JOHN ENGLER, Governor

DEPARTMENT OF STATE POLICE

BYRON WILLIAMS

RE: Order/Disposition: STALKING PERSONAL PROTECTION
Entered on: 06/19/2000
Entered by: CT
Court issued: CT

On the date listed above, an order or disposition was entered into the Law Enforcement Information Network (LEIN). This order or disposition may prohibit you from obtaining a license to purchase a pistol and shall prohibit you from obtaining a license to carry a pistol concealed.

There may be additional firearm restrictions contained in this order or disposition that are not reflected in this notice.

If you wish to contest or question the entry you must contact the court that issued the order or disposition. If you have any questions regarding which court issued the order or dispositon please contact the agency that made the LEIN entry.

You may request the State Police to delete the record if you are not the person identified in the court order or disposition or to amend any inaccurate information in LEIN. You may do so by providing a written request and supporting documentation to your nearest State Police Post. Do not send requests to this office, since only the local post has authority to make these changes.

This information has been sent to you as required by Michigan Compiled Laws Annotated (MCLA) and does not imply any attempt to purchase or obtain a license to carry a pistol.

Michigan State Police

A PROUD tradition of SERVICE through EXCELLENCE, INTEGRITY, and COURTESY

www.msp.state.mi.us

Paul Rosenberg's restraining order–part of his continual attempts to taint my name. I hadn't communicated with Paul since December 30, 1999.

Law office of:

Barton W. Morris, Jr.

ATTORNEY & COUNSELOR

May 8, 2000

Byron Williams

Re: Mathers v. Willimas
Oakland County Circuit Court Case No. :

Dear Mr. Williams,

Enclosed please find true copies of an amended Personal Protection Order and an Order on Motion to Modify Personal Protection Order. The originals have been filed with the Oakland County Clerk's Office who also entered the amendment with the Law Enforcement Information Network.

If you have any questions or concerns, please feel free to call me at your convenience.

Sincerely,

Barton W. Morris, Jr.

Enclosure

The letter from my attorney stating that my CCW permits and security license are reinstated. This was a long battle fought with Slim and Paul.

Original - Court
3rd copy - Petitioner (pink)
1st copy - Law enforcement agency (file) (green)
4th copy - Return (yellow)
2nd copy - Respondent (blue)
5th copy - Return (goldenrod)

STATE OF MICHIGAN 6TH JUDICIAL CIRCUIT OAKLAND COUNTY	A PERSONAL PROTECTION ORDER AGAINST STALKING (NON DOMESTIC) ___ EX PARTE	B CASE NO. [redacted]

Court Address 1200 Noth Telegraph Road, Pontiac, MI 48341
Court telephone no.(248)858-100[illegible]

ORI
MI-

C	Petitioner's name MARSHALL MATHERS	V	Respondent's name Williams, Byron
	Address and telephone no. where court can reach Petitioner		Address and telephone no. where court can reach Respondent

D	Full name of respondent (type or print) * BYRON WILLIAMS				Social Security no. (if known)		Driver's license number (if known)	
	Height	Weight	Race *	Sex *	Date of birth or Age *	Hair color	Eye color	Other identifying information
	6'7"	330	BLACK	M	29	BALD	BROWN	

*these items must be filled in for the police/sheriff to enter on LEIN; the other items are not required but are helpful

Date: APR 12 2000 Judge: COLLEEN A. O'BRIEN

1. This order is entered _ without a hearing. xx after hearing. Bar no.

THE COURT FINDS:

2. A petition requesting an order to restrain conduct prohibited under MCL 750.411h and 750.411i has been filed under the authority of MCL 600.2950a.

X 3. The petitioner requested an ex parte order. An ex parte order should be entered without notice because irreparable injury, loss, or damage will result from the delay required to give notice or the notice itself will precipitate adverse action before the order can be issued.

IT IS ORDERED:

4. BYRON WILLIAMS (Full name of respondent) is prohibited from stalking as defined under MCL 750.411h and MCL 750.411i which includes but is not limited to::
   - XX following or appearing within sight of the petitioner.
   - XX appearing at the workplace or residence of the petitioner.
   - XX approaching or confronting the petitioner in a public place or on private property.
   - XX entering onto or remaining on property owned, leased, or occupied by the petitioner.
   - XXsending mail/other communications to the petitioner.
   - XX contacting the petitioner by telephone.
   - XX placing an object on or delivering an object to property owned, leased, or occupied by the petitioner.
   - XX threatening to kill or physically injure the petitioner.

5. Violation of this order subjects the respondent to immediate arrest and to the civil and criminal contempt powers of the court. If found guilty, respondent shall be imprisoned for not more than 93 days and may be fined not more than $500.00.
6. This order is effective when signed, enforceable immediately, and remains in effect until December 30, 2000. This order is enforceable anywhere in the United States by any law enforcement agency under the Full Faith and Credit Act provisions of the Violence Against Women's Act.
7. The court clerk shall file this order with Oakland County Sherriff's Department/Oakland County Clerk's Office (Name of law enforcement agency), who shall enter it in the LEIN system.
8. Respondent may file a motion to modify or rescind this order. Forms and instructions are available from the clerk of the court.
9. A motion to extend the order must be filed 28 days before the expiration date below or else a new petition must be filed.
10. Other:

COLLEEN A. O'BRIEN

Date and time issued Judge

A TRUE COPY
G. WILLIAM CADDELL
Oakland County Clerk Register of Dee[ds]
Deput[y]

CC 380 (9/98) PERSONAL PROTECTION ORDER AGAINST STALKING (NON DOMESTIC)
MCL 600.2950a; MSA 27A.2950a, MCR 3.705, MCR 3.70[illegible]

The "real Slim Shady" files restraining orders!

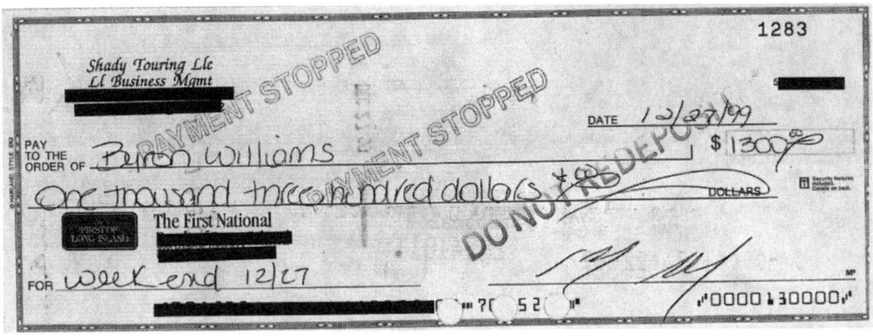

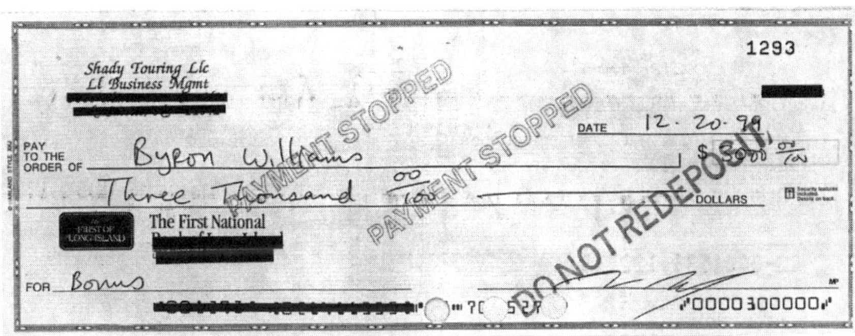

Here are two of three checks canceled by Paul Rosenberg and Slim Shady because I resigned. This ruined my family's Christmas holiday. This is part of what incited this book.

Slim and I find a way to relax after the fourteen-hour layover in Washington, DC. For a while, we had a great time.

Kim and Slim in a "Kodak moment" during the first trip to Hawaii.